The Christmas Tree Mystery

Also by Wylly Folk St. John

The Secrets of Hidden Creek

The Secrets of the Pirate Inn

The Mystery of the Gingerbread House

Illustrated by
George Porter

The
Christmas Tree
Mystery

Wylly Folk St. John

The Viking Press
New York

This book, with love,
is for the real Elizabeth
and Margaret

Contents

Elizabeth
Has to Solve
a Mystery

"Margaret!" Beth said urgently.

She closed the door to their room behind her and flung herself on her bed, flattening her face in the small, soft pillow that always seemed softer to her than anybody else's pillow because she had been using it ever since she was a baby, and that was twelve years ago. Her voice came out muffled, she noticed with a separate, surprised part of her mind. "Margaret. I've got trouble. Sure-enough trouble. I've done something awful, and I've got to try to make it right. Only I don't know if I can. I don't know how."

When you were in trouble you had to tell somebody, and now Maggie was the only person Beth could tell. Mama was almost always with Champ these days—she was never by herself in her room any more, so you could talk to her.

Beth meant for Maggie to know it was serious. In their private code, whenever she said "Margaret" instead of "Maggie" it was like saying "I need your help." Only more serious.

It was afternoon of the day before the day before Christmas. Maggie put down the red strip of paper and the green strip of paper she had been linking to add to her chain for the Christmas tree and gave the right response, the full name one. "Elizabeth?" That meant, O.K., here I am if you need me. After all, she was ten and a half now. Only two years younger than Beth.

Maybe Maggie can't help, really, Beth thought in despair. But she could listen. And there was one thing about Maggie that Beth could count on—she was loyal to her sister. Almost as loyal as Little Dog, who was lying at Maggie's feet carefully tearing up the bottom link in the paper chain. Now he jumped up on the bed and licked the back of Elizabeth's neck.

Maggie said earnestly, "So what's the matter—Elizabeth?" Beth turned her head on the pillow enough to open one eye. Maggie looked worried. Beth sat upright.

"Margaret, I said it was Pete Abel who stole them. I—I was so sure. And now I'm afraid I might have been wrong. It might not have been Pete after all. At least, Trace says it couldn't have been, because—Of course, I don't believe everything old Trace says. But this time—well, it's kind of bad. Being Christmas and all. I mean, to be so sure I saw Pete Abel, and to tell everybody he was the one."

"You mean, it wasn't Pete who stole our Christmas tree ornaments?" Maggie said incredulously. "But how would Trace know? He wasn't even here when you came home yesterday and found the stuff gone off the tree and saw Pete running out of the back yard. You saw him."

"I—I thought for sure it was Pete. I was positive." Mama always said that was Beth's main fault, the one she had to work on hardest—being so sure about things without really knowing. Jumping to conclusions, Mama called it.

"You haven't told me what Trace said."

"He said Pete was somewhere else—a good way from here—right at that time when I saw the—the thief in our yard," Beth said.

Maggie already knew all about what had happened yesterday, of course. Everybody had been away—even Pip, the baby, their little stepsister who was only three. Mama had taken her to the shopping center to see Santa Claus. Their stepfather, Champ, was at work; their thirteen-year-old stepbrother Trace was probably where he usually stayed, at what he called his "lab" in the old railroad tank tower. Maggie was at her best friend Beverly Ann's house, and Beth was walking home with her own best friend, Jane, from a Christmas party at Connie's. Beth was feeling happy and—well, satisfied about Christmas; everyone she and Jane specially liked had been at the party. She loved everybody, the way you ought to at Christmas. She'd even have tried to love Trace if he would have let her.

It was almost dark; most of the houses in the little

town already had their Christmas lights turned on. Jane, who had been walking her bike as far as the Carltons' to keep Beth company, had hopped on it then and said good-by and pedaled on toward her own house, calling back that she'd phone after supper. Beth had waved O.K., and then had stood a minute outside their big, old-fashioned, gray house until Jane turned the corner.

She was admiring the blobs of hazy-bright blue and green and red and yellow that shone like electric jewels through the twilight and fog, making every house on the street gay and welcoming for Christmas. Except theirs. Nobody was home yet to turn on the lights in the Carltons' house.

Beth and Jane and Connie still thought of Beth's home as the Carltons', though her mother had been married to Champ for nearly a year; Daddy had been dead for more than three years. She would never think of their house as the Eddisons' house, she knew, although she had to admit to herself that it was home to the Eddisons now too. Champ and Trace and Pip all lived here with them now. She loved Pip a lot, and she could try to be fair and believe that Champ was doing his best to be good to her and Maggie. But she wasn't sure about Trace. Trace seemed to be mad all the time about something. Mad at everybody, not just Mama.

Beth could understand how you might hate the thought of somebody else taking your own mother's place if your own mother was dead. Beth wouldn't let Champ take Daddy's place, ever. But she wasn't mad at Champ because she was sad about Daddy. She made it a point to remember Daddy all the time—how he looked and how his voice sounded. Remembering was a way of keeping him alive somewhere. Beth wished she could tell Trace how comforting it was to remember on purpose, every night before she went to sleep, the kiss Daddy had always given her as he said good night. That way she would never forget how it had been to have Daddy there, if she saw him in her mind, every night. So every single bedtime, she said silently, "Good night, Daddy," and he was there the way he used to be, for a minute. And she could sleep.

But it seemed as if Trace didn't want to remember his mother, and Beth couldn't get through to him, to tell him about Daddy. The first time after the Eddisons had come to live with them that she had said something sympathetic about his mother, he had shouted at her, sort of fierce and mean, "She's dead, you hear? Dead! And I don't want to talk about her. My dad promised he wouldn't, or I wouldn't have agreed to—to live here. I'd have run away when he got married again—and he knew I meant it. And I won't have anybody else talking about her. So shut up."

Trace even acted mad, most of the time, at his own father, as if it were Champ's fault that his mother was gone. Beth thought Trace might have tried harder to understand why Champ had married Mama—so Pip could have a mother, Beth supposed. Pip was too little for it to make any difference which mother she had.

So the night before, after Jane had pedaled away on her bike, Beth had hurried into the house—she didn't need a key; nobody ever locked doors in Pleasant Grove, Georgia—to turn on the lights of their own outdoor Christmas tree. She conceded, deep down in herself, that they'd never have got the lights on it and the big white lighted star all the way to the top of the cedar, without Champ. That dreadful first Christmas after Daddy died—and even last year—there had been nobody to fix the Christmas lights. Even the tree in the living room hadn't had lights, because, though Mama tried, she couldn't get them to work right, and she didn't want to let anybody help her because that would mean somebody else was taking Daddy's place. Then Mama had fallen in love with Champ, and she didn't seem to think about that any more.

Beth explored her own feeling about the Christmas lights—it was sort of like touching a sore place with your hand and finding it wasn't as sore as you thought after all; the scab was beginning to come off. She found she wasn't really sad about the Christmas lights any more; she was even a little bit glad. It was nice to have the outdoor tree lighted again.

She had pushed the button in the hall, and the cedar's electric rubies and emeralds and sapphires suddenly glowed on, brilliant in the gray dusk of the front yard. The hall light made the holly wreath on the glassed door glow too. It looked great. Beth had helped Mama make that wreath. The sleigh bells hanging from the red ribbon rang out musically when she closed the door.

Beth went quickly into the living room to plug in the lights of the indoor tree and the electric candle in the window. Champ had said that the last person to leave the house should unplug the lights, not just turn them off, so the place would be safe from fire in case of a short circuit. He didn't want to bother the Volunteer Fire Department this close to Christmas, he said. Funny, Beth thought, Daddy had always wanted the lights disconnected too. She could remember.

She turned on a table lamp and plugged in the tree lights. They were the twinkle kind—some were slower to light than others; it was like singing "Row, Row, Row Your Boat" as a round in school. About the third time around, when the blue bulbs at the back of the tree were lighting up at the same time as the green ones in front, Beth noticed that something looked wrong. It took a minute for her to figure out what it was.

"My angel—" she said out loud. "My angel's gone!"

Ever since Beth had made that angel in the first grade, it had always been put at the very top of their indoor Christmas tree. The outside tree had the Star of

Bethlehem on top; the inside one, Beth's angel. She was a beautiful pipe-cleaner-bodied angel with a shiny-green paper robe, lace wings cut from a paper doily, angel-hair around her sweet little painted face, and a halo made of a gold-sprayed pipe cleaner twisted into a circle, above her head. She was getting a bit shabby now, but nothing else would be right for the top of the tree, ever.

And now she was gone.

Beth began to search the lower branches and the floor, in case the angel had fallen.

It was then that she saw what else was wrong.

The tree was practically bare. It had the lights, all right, that was why she hadn't noticed at first that there were hardly any ornaments left on it, not even the tinsel ropes and the foil icicles and the angel-hair snow.

Somebody had practically stripped their Christmas tree. Even the valuable ornaments that Champ had got in Germany when he was in the Army while Trace was still a baby, the ornaments that had been used on the Eddisons' Christmas tree all those years and that Champ had brought with him to their new home here— even those had been stolen. And they were really worth something. The thief could sell those for real money, Beth told herself worriedly. But her angel—he might even throw that away when he looked at it in a good light. He might not think it was worth keeping. Good thing we didn't have the presents under the tree yet, she had thought even while she was wondering wildly what to do.

Here in their room the next day, telling Maggie about how Trace had given Pete an alibi, Beth felt sort of hopeless about ever seeing her angel again.

Maggie was saying, "Tell me again why you thought it was Pete. And where did Trace say he was?"

"That's just it—he won't tell that part. He won't say where it was he saw Pete. He says it might get Pete in more trouble, and he doesn't think it's fair to get him in any more trouble than he just naturally gets himself in."

"So tell me," Maggie said, "about when you saw Pete in the back yard."

Beth told her again, though she had already told it over and over. She had felt a cold draft on her neck right after she saw the ornaments were all gone, and had figured that maybe whoever stole them had just opened the back door to get away. Maybe the thief still had been in the house when she came in the front door. Maybe she could catch him.

Without stopping to feel scared, she rushed through the back hall into the family room. The door to the back yard stood open, blown wide by gusts of cold December air. Beth pressed the button that turned on the floodlight for the drive.

A tall boy wearing an old Army jacket was just disappearing around the corner of the woodshed. She

could see only his back and his light hair, but she knew who it was—the only boy it was likely to be. It had to be. The worst boy in town. "Pete Abel!" she screamed. "You come right back here with my angel!"

The boy got away. Later, when Champ came home and she told him, he and the police chief went to ask Pete about it. Of course, Pete denied being anywhere in the neighborhood. Well, he would. Chief Steadman, who was one-third of the town's police force, had known Pete for years and couldn't overlook the boy's reputation for always being in some kind of trouble. So the Chief had assured Champ that it was bound to have been Pete, all right, no matter what he said. They'd make him admit it, sooner or later, and get the things back.

Champ had said to forget it; Christmas was no time to be prosecuting a kid for stealing Christmas tree ornaments. Maybe Pete had smaller brothers and sisters and nothing to put on their tree; maybe it wasn't just vandalism. Chief Steadman said No, that Pete didn't have any small kids in his family and that he probably had done it just for devilment. And that if they let him get away with it this time, it'd be something worse next time. Champ had said he hoped the boy would decide to confess, but that he wouldn't take any action against him right now, because after all there wasn't any real evidence.

But Beth wanted her angel back. Pete—or whoever

took the ornaments—could have the rest of the things; Champ would buy some more. (But he couldn't ever buy any like the German ones, unless he went back to Germany. There was a spun-glass nest with a gilded bird, a marvelous bird that could sing, and pine cones with real silver filigree.)

"I need that angel," she said now, emphatically.

Maggie nodded; she understood how it was when you had made your own angel. "He could have those chains I made, if he needed some for their tree," she said. "I don't mind that he took those. I can always make more; I make chains better than anything. But your angel is special."

Beth got off the bed and smoothed her pillow and spread, then moved restlessly to the window, followed by Little Dog. "But anyhow, now it seems that maybe Pete didn't do it. So we don't have any clue about who's got it and the rest of the stuff."

"Except that old crumpled-up handkerchief that whoever it was dropped accidentally under the tree," Maggie reminded her.

"That's another thing—it didn't have Pete Abel's initial on it. The initial was *Z*, remember?" Beth said reluctantly. "I guess it's really the only clue we have to the criminal."

"Pete probably doesn't ever carry a handkerchief anyhow," Maggie said realistically. "Not even a dirty one. He probably wipes his nose on his sleeve."

"But whoever stole the things did have on an Army jacket like Pete wears all the time. And the light shone on his hair and it looked kind of blond like Pete's. At least it wasn't dark."

"Still, lots of the kids wear old Army jackets now," Maggie pointed out. "Even girls. I wish I had one, but Trace won't even let me wear Champ's one time. Of course, it's just to keep warm that Pete Abel wears that old one I bet the Salvation Army gave him. But Mike bought one just like it at the Army surplus store, because Army jackets are In. Roderick and Alan bought them, too. And Ben."

"Well, it just couldn't have been any of them," Beth said positively. "At least, I don't think it could," she amended, conscientiously trying not to be so sure of everything without any good reason. Mama had said she ought to practice not jumping to conclusions. "None of them has a name that begins with Z—not a first name nor a last name. But now it looks like it couldn't have been Pete, either. I guess I won't ever see my angel again."

Her voice was mournful. She leaned down and pulled Little Dog's floppy honey-colored ears, noticing that the cocker spaniel was almost the same color as Maggie's hair. Beth had brown hair and eyes, but Maggie was a honey blonde with gray eyes. Beth was obscurely glad she herself resembled Daddy's side of the family; nobody could think she was an Eddison.

They might mistake Maggie for Pip's and Trace's real sister, because of their hair, but not dark Beth.

"Wonder why Trace won't tell where it was he saw Pete?" Maggie said, mystified. "It couldn't get him in any more trouble with Chief Steadman than he is now."

"What I think is," Beth answered, "maybe old Trace is afraid it'll get old Trace in trouble if he admits being there himself—wherever it was he saw Pete."

"Aw, he wasn't anywhere but in his lab. It's not as if he was a friend of Pete's. He's not. Trace isn't friends with any of the kids, you know that. He wasn't anywhere with Pete. I saw him going toward the lab—by himself—when I was ringing Beverly Ann's doorbell about an hour or two before then."

"That old lab!" Beth sniffed.

"You just don't like it because Trace won't let us go up there," Maggie surmised shrewdly. "Maybe you're jealous," she teased.

Beth thought that over, trying to be fair. "Could be," she admitted. "Maybe I do wish Mr. Marvell had given us the key to that neat old tower, instead of taking a shine to Trace and giving it to him. Oh, it would have been so great to fix it up! For a clubhouse or something. Whenever I looked at those little windows up there, I used to think about putting curtains in them. Only three blocks from home too."

"Why didn't we think to ask Mr. Marvell about it

then?" Maggie said. "Before Trace got here. Before Champ even came from Oklahoma to Pleasant Grove to run the new mill, we could've asked Mr. Marvell and maybe he would have let us use the old tower. It's right across that big old field from Ginny's grandma's house—maybe Ginny would have asked him for us, if we'd thought of it first. Now it's too late."

"No—we're girls. I'm practically certain Mr. Marvell would've thought it was dangerous for girls to climb up there." Beth sighed wistfully.

The structure that looked like a high old tower was beside the railroad tracks, a short distance up the rails from the depot where Mr. Marvell was station agent. He was almost eighty now and thinking about retiring; he had been station agent there since long before World War II. The tower had been built during the War, Trace said. It was a big tank of concrete, nearly a hundred feet high, he guessed. It had been needed then for storing diesel oil to refuel the troop trains before they got into Atlanta, forty miles away. At the top of the tank, away from the oil chute, there was a little narrow platform with a frame hut on it, like a penthouse, where the man who put the oil in the engines had stayed at night; sometimes he had had to stoke up engines half a dozen times a night.

Up there was kind of like being in a forest ranger's lookout tower or a lighthouse, Trace said. The wallboarded room had a cot and an electric hot plate and plumbing; and Mr. Marvell had turned on the water and lights so Trace could use it as a lab. Trace said he needed electricity for his experiments. Mr. Marvell had even lent him an electric heater. Wooden stairs zigzagging up the cylindrical tank led to the lab. The stairs looked rotten but were safe enough, Trace said, for a boy; but he told the girls not to dare set a foot on any plank of them. The oil storage tank and hut had been unused for years; there were only two trains a day through Pleasant Grove now, and the depot was closed at night. That room at the top of the tower was just the place for a scientific boy's lab—a boy who made friends with an old man instead of with other boys.

"If we had let Mr. Marvell teach us the wireless code," Maggie said, "he might have liked us too." The station agent had drilled Trace in telegraphy, and he was so good at it that he could send messages from the top of the tower with a Boy Scout whistle, and Mr. Marvell would answer them from the depot with another whistle. Maggie thought that was cool, but Beth kind of agreed with Champ when he muttered about Trace's childishness. Trace said he and Mr. Marvell were going to make him a regular wireless sending and receiving set as soon as Mr. Marvell had time.

"We aren't 'brilliant' like Trace," Beth answered scornfully, envying him in spite of her good resolutions not to. "Everybody thinks Trace is so smart, with all that chemical stuff of his and his silly electrical experiments and all. I bet he short-circuits himself some day."

"Well, he is pretty smart," Maggie said, defending him. "Look how many things he did with the motor from Mama's old vacuum cleaner and with that old TV set he took apart too."

Beth could tell that her sister sort of liked Trace—Maggie had always wanted a big brother. Sometimes Beth wished Maggie could remember better, back to when Daddy was alive and everything was different and there wasn't any old boy living in the house with them.

"There you go, taking up for him when I'm so miserable," she said. Little Dog prudently went back to Maggie.

"Miserable? Why are you? So—Trace says Pete didn't do it. Well, it's up to Chief Steadman to find out who did, that's all. It's not your problem. You're not in any trouble that I can see."

"You don't understand." Beth groaned. "They all believe what I said. That it was Pete I saw. Champ and Chief Steadman and Mama and everybody. Even though I told them what Trace said, and he told them too. Because Pete is the worst boy in town, they believed me instead of him. That means Pete's in big trouble. And Trace won't say where he saw Pete, so they think Trace is just sorry for him and trying to give him an alibi. So the alibi won't hold up unless Trace tells where he saw Pete."

"So why are you in trouble?"

"Because," Beth explained worriedly, "I broke one of the Ten Commandments, that's why. That was bearing false witness, is what it was. So I just can't let them go on thinking it was Pete when it wasn't. Even if he is the worst boy in town. And Trace did sound as if he was telling the truth. I believe him about that—even if I don't always believe everything he says. He looked all right when he said it—you know how it always shows, if it's true or not? I guess it was his eyes. They looked true, when he said it couldn't have been Pete. So—" she said impressively, "you and I, Margaret, have got to find out who really stole the things off the Christmas tree. Or I can't have a good Christmas at all, not if they're still blaming Pete because I accused him."

"Tomorrow's Christmas Eve," Maggie said, shaking her head. "I don't believe we can find out by then. Besides, I have to make some more chains for our poor tree."

"Champ's going to buy new ornaments. But I'll help you with the chains, if you'll help me. First, though," she said, dragging the words out with reluctant dread, "I guess I've got to go and find Pete Abel and tell him I'm sorry I thought he was the one. And I bet he's got it in for me, for getting him in trouble. I'm kind of scared even to go over there where he lives."

"I'll go with you—Elizabeth," Margaret said.

She looked serious—and sweet, Beth thought. She hugged Maggie, suddenly. "Thanks, Margaret."

When Maggie stood up, Little Dog ran to his corner and got his leash, bringing it to her in his mouth.

"Little Dog'll go too. He'll protect us," Maggie said, patting his head while he wriggled ecstatically.

"I wonder," Beth mused, "I wonder whose name around here begins with a *Z*?"

"Nobody's," Maggie said, snapping the leash onto Little Dog's collar and turning over in her mind the names of people she knew in Pleasant Grove. "I don't believe there's anybody in this whole town whose name begins with a *Z*. First name or last name."

"We don't know everybody," Beth said.

"We can look in the phone book," Maggie suggested.

Beth drew a deep breath. "Yes. But first let's go see if I can apologize to Pete. It's the hardest thing I've ever had to do, though."

"He can't do anything to us."

"All he can do is kill us, that's all."

"In that case," Maggie said thoughtfully, "we'd better leave a note to tell Mama where to pick up our bodies."

The
One Clue
Disappears

The wind blew Little Dog's dangling ears inside out as the girls crossed the main street. The day was raw and gray, with clouds hanging low.

"It's cold," Beth said, shivering. "I'm glad we got Little Dog a sweater for Christmas."

"Sh-sh-sh," Maggie said. "He'll hear you, and we were going to surprise him and let him think Santa Claus brought it, remember?"

"I don't think he heard me." Little Dog was pulling at his leash, trying to get close enough to Beverly Ann's brother Ben's dog Pup to rub noses. "Ben must be around here somewhere," Beth surmised. "Or Pup wouldn't be loose."

"He's probably in the ten-cent store, doing his Christmas shopping. That dog goes everywhere after Ben the way Useless follows Pip." Useless was Pip's black-and-white cat. They had been babies together, and Useless had come with the Eddisons. Beth didn't like cats much. She hardly ever even patted Useless.

"And that reminds me," Maggie said, "we ought to get Useless a Christmas present too."

"You get him one."

All the store windows were decorated for Christmas, and at any other time Maggie and Beth would have walked up one side of the street and down the other, lingering before every window, enjoying the tinselly season. The wind was waving the garlands of pine draped around the lampposts, and pulling at the strings of lights that hung, concealed by greenery, high above the street, crisscrossing it. The holly trees in big tubs along the edges of the sidewalks on both sides of the street had decorations on them too.

"This town is all ready for Christmas," Maggie remarked with satisfaction. "And I'll buy old Useless a cat collar. The kind that unsnaps instead of choking him if he gets caught going through a wire fence or gets hung up on a bush or anything. I've some of my Christmas money left. He can think Santa Claus brought it. Pip can too."

"We can't stop to look at things now," Beth said, frowning. Then she relented. After all, it was Christmas time. "Maybe on the way home, though."

"How do you know where Pete Abel lives, anyhow?" Maggie said.

"Jane told me. Jane knows everything. We discuss things."

"Beverly Ann and I discuss things, too," Maggie

said thoughtfully. "But never things like Pete Abel."

"Jane says it's scandalous for the Abels to live in an old railroad car like they do," Beth went on. "They must have found it in some old railroad graveyard."

"You mean like an elephant graveyard?" Maggie giggled. "Where old railroad trains go to die?"

"Well, not exactly. Probably a dump pile. Maybe the railroad gave it to them. Maybe Mr. Marvell got it for them because they didn't have any house to live in. Jane says it's scandalous that Pete's father won't work. She says anybody in Pleasant Grove can get a job at the mill if he wants to work. I know Champ would give him a job. And then they could live in a decent house of their own, or at the Project."

"So why doesn't his mother get a job at the mill? Some people's mothers do."

"He hasn't got any mother. His sister does the cooking and all."

"Are there any kids besides Pete and his sister?"

"I don't know. Not in my class at school."

"Mine either. Chief Steadman said no small ones."

They had crossed the railroad bridge and were on an unpaved street now that ran beside the railroad tracks beyond the lab. Soon there were no houses. Little Dog trotted ahead, his ears still catching the breeze; Pup had stayed behind to wait for Ben close to the store's entrance, as he always did when Ben was inside anywhere. The stores were right over there, only a couple of blocks away on the other side of the tracks, yet to the girls it seemed as lonely as if they had been way out in the country.

"There's a bunch of trees," Beth said. "They probably parked the railroad car back there, away from everybody else. It's kind of like living in a trailer, I guess."

"I hope we get to see inside it," Maggie said. "Do you realize we've never even been on a railroad train at all? We've only seen inside railroad cars in movies."

"It won't have seats like a train now," Beth told her. "It'll have beds and things."

"I sure hope we get to see that. Beds in a train! A stove too, I'll bet."

"There are regular trains too that have beds, but they fold up," Beth said. "They're called Pullmans. Daddy rode in one once when he went to New York."

"There it is!" Maggie said. "And they've got a fire going. Look at the smoke coming out of that—well, it's not exactly a chimney, is it? It's a smoke pipe, I guess, stuck through the roof."

The old railroad car was set up off the ground on cement blocks; the wheels were gone. The glass was gone too from some of the windows, and cardboard had been tacked across them. There was a cement block to step onto in order to reach the metal stairs leading to the platform, which had an old porch chair on it and some clothes—jeans and underwear and towels—drying on the rail. It wasn't much of a house, Beth thought. But Maggie was staring as if she were enchanted.

"It must be fun to live in a railroad car," she said.

"It's different, all right," Beth agreed.

A voice startled them. "What are you staring at?"

It was Pete Abel, belligerent as usual. He came around the back of the railroad car with an armload of wood split up to burn. He was wearing the old Army jacket and some ragged jeans, and his longish blond hair was waving in the wind just like Little Dog's ears, Maggie noticed. He had a hatchet stuck in his belt, and he looked real tough.

"Nothing," Maggie said automatically.

Well, I blew it, she thought. He'll never ask us in, now. Maybe if we'd said the right thing—

"We came—" Beth said, and swallowed hard. "Margaret and I—"

It was an appeal for help. Maggie answered it. "Elizabeth and I—we came to tell you—"

"That I'm sorry," Beth finished the sentence in a rush. "I'm sorry I thought it was you. Because Trace says you were somewhere else. So you couldn't have been the one who took the things off our Christmas tree. But unless you'll tell where you were—Trace won't tell —unless you will, well, they won't believe that you weren't the one. So you see—"

"So I'm in trouble, and it's your fault," Pete said bluntly.

"I said I'm sorry."

"Elizabeth is very sorry," Maggie added earnestly.

"So what are you going to do about it?"

"If you'll tell us where you really were last night just before suppertime, I'll convince them," Beth offered. "If anybody else saw you, it'd help out the alibi. Trace said he wouldn't tell because it might get you in more trouble."

"Huh. He couldn't have known where I was. Wasn't anybody else there at all."

"Where?"

"I'm not about to tell anybody. He's right about that. It'd get me in more trouble. But I'll tell you where I wasn't. I wasn't at your house."

Beth looked hopeless. Maggie slipped a hand into hers and squeezed it. That was all she could think of to do.

Just then the back door of the railroad car—the door to the platform—opened and a girl's voice said, "Aren't you all freezing out there? Why don't you come in?"

"Sure," Maggie said happily, starting toward the car. But Beth held back.

"Who's that?" she asked.

"It's my sister Goldie," Pete said. He called to her, "No, they gotta go." He scowled.

Goldie came out on the platform, shivering in a thin sweater, and the girls saw that she was older, nearly grown-up.

"Oh, I guess we could go in for a minute," Maggie

said to Pete hopefully. She smiled at Goldie and told her, "I'm Margaret Carlton and this is my sister Elizabeth. But you can call us Maggie and Beth if you want to."

"Oh," Goldie said. Beth could see her remembering Chief Steadman's visit to accuse Pete and to say Beth saw him. Goldie didn't look quite so friendly now.

"I came to—to apologize to Pete," Beth told his sister. "But he won't accept my apology."

Maggie was halfway up the car's steps by now, with Little Dog ahead of her, and Beth couldn't let them go in alone; so she followed. But before they could go in-

side they were halted by a shout from the edge of the woods.

"Don't you go in there!"

A boy came running toward the railroad car. Little Dog jerked loose and leaped to meet him. It was Trace. He brushed past Pete Abel, leaped onto the car steps and pulled Maggie and Beth roughly down to the ground again. "You come on home," he ordered.

"Are you out of your mind, Trace Eddison?" Beth said. She was really kind of glad for an excuse to get away, but she couldn't let Trace think he could order her around as if he were her brother.

"How did you know where we were, anyhow, to follow us?" Maggie asked. She stepped on the end of the leash and then picked it up, heeling Little Dog.

"I read the note you left on the kitchen table for Aunt Mary, that's how." He called his stepmother "Aunt Mary"; Beth didn't blame him for not calling her "Mama." "And they weren't home, and I knew you shouldn't—Well, you just come on home, that's all. You two need a keeper."

"Well, you don't have to be responsible for us." Beth stuck out her chin and defied him. "You leave us alone and we'll leave you alone, O.K.?"

Maggie said softly, "It was kind of nice of Trace to care about looking after us—"

"I didn't care!" he retorted. "You're not my real sisters. I just didn't want you to come over here and get into some kind of a mess about that Christmas tree stuff. I told you he didn't do it because I know he was somewhere else. So you keep out of it."

Pete said, "Yeah, and what I want to know is, how did you know where I was?" He dropped the wood he had been holding all this time, and strode up to Trace as if he meant to knock the answer out of him.

Goldie said, "Pete, you come in here right now." But Pete didn't pay any attention to his sister. She went back inside—probably because she was cold, Beth guessed. She noticed that the boys were about the same size, and she wondered if Pete could actually beat Trace up. She didn't much think he could; Trace could probably hold his own. But that would be on Beth's conscience too, if they hurt each other.

"Look, it's not going to do anybody any good to fight about it," she said hastily. "If neither one of you is willing to make Pete's alibi sound reasonable to Chief Steadman by telling where he actually was, then the only way to solve this mystery is for us to find out who really took the stuff. Why don't we all work together and try to find the criminal? I'll bet we can do it quicker than the Chief, because he believes his theory about Pete's doing it, and we know that's wrong. So we're way ahead of him already."

Trace thought that over and agreed reluctantly, "Well, if you kids will come on home right now and not give me any more trouble, I'll have to do what you want me to, to help you, I guess."

Pete said rudely, "Not me. It wasn't me and I don't want to be mixed up in it any more than you've mixed me up in it already. But if you don't clear me with Chief Steadman and everybody—" He left the threat hanging ominously in the air.

"I told you I'm sorry," Beth said. "But I'll find out who really took the ornaments, and then they'll believe me. Even if you won't help."

"You'd better." Pete picked up the wood again and

went into the railroad car without even saying good-by.

"Come on home," Trace repeated.

As they started on the road toward town, Maggie said, "I do wish we could've gone inside. His sister seemed pretty nice, at first."

"It's not safe," Trace said gruffly. "Probably his old man is lying around in there drunk or something. No telling what would've happened to you. You're girls, and girls have got to be careful where they go."

"We had Little Dog," Maggie said meekly. Little Dog wagged his tail when he heard his name.

"Nothing was going to happen to us," Beth said scornfully. "If I didn't need all the help I can get to solve this mystery, Trace Eddison, I'd just tell you to mind your own business!"

"Why don't you just forget the whole thing?" Trace said. "It's nearly Christmas Eve. Dad and Aunt Mary were going to the shopping center to get new ornaments. They said we all have to help decorate the tree again tonight. You haven't really got time to try to find out who took the other ornaments."

"Pete Abel is so hateful, I ought not to worry about it," Beth said. "But I do. If I hadn't said it was Pete, I wouldn't care who it was. But I don't feel good inside about people thinking it was Pete, just because he's been in trouble before. It's not fair. Didn't you ever," she asked Trace, "have a kind of sick feeling in your stomach, like you'd swallowed a heavy rock or something, because of something you did, until you made it right again?"

Trace didn't even answer; she could tell he thought she was being stupid. Well, all right, maybe boys were different.

They were back on the main street now. "Let me get that Christmas present for Useless," Maggie said. "I brought my money."

"What are you buying him?" Trace asked. He sounded more like a brother, Beth thought, when he was talking to Maggie, than when he talked to her.

"A collar. Let's go in the ten-cent store. Have you got any money left, Trace? Would you like to help give it to him? We could get a nicer one if we both put in some money."

"I would," Trace said gruffly, "except I spent all my Christmas money last week. And an advance on my allowance that Dad lent me too. I haven't had any money for about a week. So I can't."

"Well, never mind then. You can help pick it out, anyway, since Useless is partly your cat."

"Dad and I named him, because Pip was too little."

Maggie had a hard time deciding whether to get a blue collar or a pink one, but finally decided on blue because blue was for boys, and Trace assured her Useless was a boy cat. "That's why he stays out all night sometimes," he told her. "Tomcats do."

"Why?"

"They just like to wander around, and fight, and holler at other cats. I wouldn't be surprised if Useless got his tail chewed off sometime."

"Why don't we keep him in the house, so he couldn't get into fights?"

"Aw, he'd rather take his chances."

"Well, I bet he'll like his collar, anyhow," Maggie said. "Hardly anybody except Pip ever pets Useless or gives him anything. And good-will-to-men means cats too, I'm pretty certain. I can't wait to see how he likes getting a present! Maybe I won't wait for Christmas— maybe I'll give it to him right now, when we get home."

As soon as they got in the door, Maggie called Pip and showed her the collar, forgetting it was to have been from Santa Claus. So then she figured she might as well go ahead and put it on Useless. It took both of them, Maggie and Pip, to get Useless in the mood to accept his Christmas present. He didn't much like wearing a collar.

While they were laughing at his efforts to get it off, Beth was still trying to think how she could find out who the criminal was. The only clue was the handkerchief dropped at the scene of the crime. She hadn't yet checked the telephone book to see if there were any Z's. She realized there were lots of people in town she didn't know, and it was possible that somebody named Zeigler or Zenith might not be listed. But she got the book and looked. It was a start. No, there wasn't anybody in it with a name that began with a *Z*. The *Y*'s were the last classification.

It was Beth's night to help Mama in the kitchen. She put the phone book back beside the phone, and went to set the table. Mama was standing at the stove, stirring mush for spoon bread.

"Mama," Beth said, "how can I find out who took the ornaments?"

"Do you have to find out? We bought more, you know."

"Well—I said it was Pete and it wasn't. His sister Goldie didn't like that, and I don't blame her. I'm going to feel awful all through Christmas, with everybody believing me instead of him, unless I can prove who it really was."

"Yes, I guess you do have to try," Mama agreed. "Maybe you could do it by the process of elimination. You saw a boy. Write down the names of all the boys who could possibly fit the description of the one you saw as to age, height, and so on, and then see if each one will tell you where he was at that time."

"They'd say it was none of my beeswax."

"If you told them why, they might not say it was none of your business. And one of them might be startled into saying something that would give you a clue. Here, stir this for me."

She went to the refrigerator and began pushing things around in it. "Where's the—" she began. Then she said unbelievingly, "Beth! There's something else missing! I had half a ham in here, and it's gone. You children didn't eat half a ham, by any chance, did you?" She checked other supplies rapidly. "And a loaf of bread's gone. And a stick of butter. A box of crackers—and I believe there were four tomatoes and now there are only two. I wonder what else they took? The bananas and oranges for the ambrosia! There were lots more of those—"

Beth said, "My clue! I wonder if it's safe—"

"What clue?" Mama said distractedly.

"The handkerchief with the Z on it that the thief dropped under the tree when he stole the ornaments. After I showed it to you all, I put it in my drawer." She handed the stirring spoon back to Mama. "Here, Mama, you stir it," she asked. "I've got to go see if it's still there."

She came rushing back downstairs, calling to Maggie, "Margaret! Margaret! Did you put it anywhere?"

Maggie stopped playing with the cat and jumped up, tumbling Pip and Useless in a heap on the rug. "Put what? What are you talking about—Elizabeth?"

"The handkerchief! The only clue we had! It's gone!"

Trace's
Secret

Champ looked serious when he heard about the new thefts, and said they were going to have to start locking the doors when nobody was to be at home.

"But goodness knows where the key is," Mama said. "We never have needed it before."

"I'll have new ones made tomorrow," Champ said.

"Why don't you get one for Trace and each of the girls, too?" Mama said. "Duplicates don't cost much."

"Oh, Mama!" Maggie said rapturously. "You mean I can have my own key, just like I was grown-up?"

"That's what I mean." Mama smiled. She looked very pretty when she smiled. "It can be a Christmas present—from The Establishment."

The Establishment was a joke of Mama's. That was what she sometimes called herself and Champ when she was making fun of herself and him for acting like parents. Or when she wanted to make a new house rule about something and didn't want it to sound as if the parents were clamping down on each other's children separately. Beth saw through the little trick, all right, but she didn't mind. She could understand that if Champ made a stern law about something she or Maggie did, it might seem that he was picking on Mama's children, or that if Mama made a rule for Trace, it might seem like picking on Champ's boy. But if The Establishment—both together—made the rule it was different. Beth thought it was a pretty good idea. Mama had a way of making family jokes that often solved a tough problem. Like, for instance, calling her new husband Champ sometimes just for fun, because, she said, he was the chess champion—he always beat her when they played. That gave Beth and Maggie something to call him besides Daddy. Mama knew they couldn't have called him that no matter how much they liked him.

"Thanks, Mama," Maggie said. "When do we get the keys? In our stockings?"

"I'll get them made first thing in the morning," Champ said. "As soon as I can get a locksmith or somebody who can fix them. We won't wait to give them to you on Christmas because we might need to lock the door tomorrow, Christmas Eve."

After supper Mama let each one choose a Christmas record to play while they fixed the tree. Mama always wanted "Carol, Carol, Christians"—it had been Daddy's favorite too. Pip decided on "Rudolph the Red-nosed Reindeer" without any trouble at all. Mag-

gie chose "O Little Town of Bethlehem"; Champ said
he'd settle for "Silent Night." Beth's was always, "It
Came Upon the Midnight Clear." In her mind the angels
bending near the earth to touch their harps of gold always looked like her shining-robed, pipe-cleaner angel.

"I'm still sad about my angel," she confided to Maggie, who was looping chains about the lower branches
of the tree. "The top of the tree doesn't look right with
that crazy pointed sparkly ornament on it."

"Well—" Maggie tried to offer some comfort. "You
can always see behind your eyes how it looked with the
angel up there. I can. If we shut our eyes and think
hard, we can just blank out the pointed ornament and
put your angel back."

"Neat," Beth said. She shut her eyes, and sure
enough, the angel was there.

"What do you think you're doing, trimming a tree
with your eyes shut?" Trace said. He hadn't chosen a
record; he said he didn't like Christmas carols.

"Just remembering," Beth said wistfully. "I've
always had my angel at the top of the tree ever since the
first grade."

The phone rang. "I'll get it!" Maggie said, and she
raced for the hall. Little Dog barked and ran with her.

She came back in a minute, looking puzzled. "It
wasn't a wrong number," she said, "because somebody
asked for Mr. William Tracey Eddison. But when I
said to wait a minute, please, and I'd call Champ, she

said No, and sort of choked, and hung up. Who do you suppose it was, Champ?"

"Oh, probably somebody from the mill," Champ said, "trying to get up nerve enough to borrow some Christmas money. If they call back, I'll answer it."

"Will you let them have it?" Maggie said hopefully.

"Of course. It's Christmas." He smiled at her, and Maggie smiled too and went back to her decorating. But the phone didn't ring again.

They worked awhile happily, with the carols soft and sweet in the background. "My favorite!" Maggie breathed when the boy choir sang "O Little Town of Bethlehem." She stopped a minute to listen, and then went back to the tree. "I do hope we've made enough chains," she said to Beth.

"Plenty," Beth said reassuringly. "They're beautiful, Maggie."

When Mama, at the top of the ladder, said, "Hand me one end of a chain, Maggie, and let me put some up toward the top too," Beth could see Maggie glow with delight because they all liked her chains. Some people wouldn't have homemade ornaments on their Christmas trees. Some people even had trees made out of aluminum foil, with nothing but silver ornaments on them. Beth was glad that this family hadn't changed from liking a real pine tree—one with short needles—and all kinds of ornaments, including homemade ones. She wished they could have real candles too, like the tree on an old-fashioned Christmas card Grandma had once shown her. That would really be neat. But too dangerous, Daddy had always said. So they had never had them.

Just as if he had read her mind, Champ said, from where he was holding the ladder and Mama to be sure she didn't fall, "We used to have real candles, when Trace was a kid. But we shouldn't have. It was a dangerous thing to do—even if I was mighty careful." He helped Mama down. "And by the way, where has Trace got to? I told him this job had priority tonight."

"Oh, if he doesn't want to do it, let him alone," Mama said. "Maybe Christmas is almost too sad a season for him, without his own mother. You know how he feels about—Well, Bill, let's face it, 'Aunt Mary' will never take her place for Trace. He's probably up there in his room suffering, hating Christmas because it's not the same without her."

"But if you loved Christmas, you'd want it to go on, even after you're dead," Beth said. "Daddy loved Christmas. I'm doing this for him too, because he can't any more."

"Right," Mama said, smiling—and blinking her eyes the way she did when she was trying not to cry.

Beth saw Maggie stop and remember, with her lips trembling as if she might cry too; so Beth said hurriedly, to change the subject, "Maybe Trace will be all right by next year. I sure hope so."

"Trace go out," Pip said.

"Oh, no, Pip," Maggie said. "He's up in his room."

There were plenty of chains; Maggie even gave Pip a little one for her doll's Christmas tree. The big tree was finished just as the records ended, and they all stood back to look at it. Little Dog didn't bother; he was snoozing by the fire. Useless was out tomcatting around somewhere; he had already sniffed at the tree and rubbed against its trunk before he left, approving it.

The twinkling lights made Mama's eyes look as if they were twinkling too. "It's just about as pretty as it was before," she said.

"Not quite," Beth said sorrowfully. But she shut her eyes, and then it was.

"I think I'll make some cocoa," Mama said, "and cut the fruitcake. Beth, come with me, and I'll fix a small tray for you to take over to Mr. Smith." He was an old man who lived all alone on the corner across from the Eddisons' and cater-cornered from Miss Carrie's. Mr. Smith didn't have much to celebrate Christmas about, but he had given Beth some of the red berries from his holly to put on her wreath, and she liked him.

"That'll be neat, Mama. But as soon as we get through eating, I've got to get busy calling those kids and asking where they were last night at twilight. Good thing they can't hit me over the phone."

Beth was coming back from Mr. Smith's, crossing
the street, when she saw Trace.

Mr. Smith had said thank you and a kind of rusty
Merry Christmas—after Beth had Merry Christmased
him first. She had already passed their outdoor lighted
tree, lifting her face to the black sky and trying to see
a star behind the clouds. At last the wind swirled a wisp
of cloud away and she glimpsed a small one. "Star
light, star bright," she murmured. "First star I've seen
tonight, Wish I may, Wish I might, Have the wish I
wish tonight." Then she said out loud, solemnly, "I wish
I could have my angel back."

It was when she turned her eyes away from the sky
toward the bright door with the holly wreath, that she
saw Trace. He wasn't going in the front door, but there
was light enough from it to let Beth see him slipping
around the corner of the house. "Hey, Trace! Where've
you been?" she called. He didn't answer. She ran after
him and caught him before he could sneak in the back
door.

"What are you doing? So Pip did see you going out,
after all."

"Nothing."

He didn't have on a coat, just a sweater, and Beth
thought she could guess why. Without a coat, he could
pretend to anybody who saw him just after he came in
that he'd been in the house all the time. The sweater
was too little for him—all his clothes were. He

wouldn't even try on the new ones Mama had bought
for him; he was still wearing the old clothes his own
mother had bought for him two years ago. The sleeves
of the sweater let his bare arms stick out about six
inches. Trace's expression was sort of odd and mixed-
up, and Beth surmised he must have been doing something he didn't want to be caught doing. Probably it
was the same thing he had been up to when he saw Pete
Abel not-robbing them—and it would get Trace in
trouble if anybody found out about it.

She was right that he didn't want to be caught, because he looked down at the ground and then said, all

in a rush as if it was hard to say, "Look, Beth, don't tell them I was out, O.K.? I don't think anybody else saw me while I was—out. I didn't let anybody see me."

Beth said, "Why should I cover up for you? What are you up to anyhow? Something mysterious—and Pete Abel said he would get in trouble if anybody knew where he was, so that means you would too."

"It's not the same. I mean, Pete wasn't with me. I just—Oh, I can't explain it to you. I can't tell anybody. But it's important—it's very important." He looked so desperate that Beth felt sorry for him.

"I'm no informer," she said loftily, picking the

word out of a spy story she had been reading. "And neither is Maggie, in case I decide to tell her, which I probably will. But if what you're up to is wrong, Trace Eddison, you had better stop it. Because, sure as my name's Elizabeth, The Establishment will find out about it. Mama always knows when we've done something wrong. I don't know how she guesses, but she does."

Trace looked mutinous. "Aunt Mary won't do anything to me. And Dad knows I'll run away if he—well, anyhow, you won't give me away? I—I'll do something for you sometime."

"Never mind." Then she had another thought. "Well, I guess you can do something for me, after all," she bargained. "I was going to call up all the boys who fit the age and size and all of the one I saw last night running away, and ask where they were at the time. It was Mama's idea. But you can do it for me. They'd be more likely to tell another boy, see? Will you?"

"Guess I'll have to," he said slowly, reluctantly. "But it's a stupid idea. Anyway, how do you know it wasn't a girl? A girl in slacks could look like a boy who wears his hair long, like Donovan's. I'll bet it was a girl."

"It wasn't that long. But girls do wear Army jackets too. I guess it could have been a girl. But then what about my instinct? My woman's intuition? That told me it was a boy."

"It told you it was Pete Abel too," Trace pointed out,

"and it was definitely wrong. So it probably was a girl."

"Well, call up girls too, if you want to."

"Not me! We made a deal. All I promised was the boys. You tell me which ones you want me to call and make a fool of myself to, and I'll do it. But that's all. Let's go in now, and don't you let on."

"O.K. They think you were up in your room. Maybe you'd better be up there. Mama will probably send Maggie to see if you want some cocoa. They're waiting for me to come back from Mr. Smith's to have it. Mama cut the fruitcake too."

"I don't like fruitcake."

"You don't like anything, do you?" Beth was sort of sorry for him, but impatient with him too. It was his own fault he wasn't having any fun this Christmas.

Useless came strolling up and slid inside between their legs when they opened the door. He still had his collar on, Beth noticed. She had been afraid he'd lose it before Christmas, and that would make Maggie unhappy.

Trace slipped past the living room door without being seen and went upstairs. Useless and Beth went on to the kitchen, where Beth gave Useless some milk and then helped Mama bring the cake and cocoa into the living room. They were all sitting around the fire, waiting for it. Sure enough, Mama said to Maggie, "Go and ask Trace if he wants some, honey."

Trace came back with Maggie. "I had to make him

come," she whispered to Beth, "but I did it. He can't resign from Christmas like he resigned from that club Alan and Roderick and Mike elected him to."

Beth said thoughtfully, "They all have dark hair. Tell me the names of all the boys about the size of Pete Abel that you can think of, Maggie, that have blond hair. I'm going to find out if they all have alibis for the time our tree was robbed. That is, old Trace is going to do it for me."

"No!" Maggie said, unbelieving. "How in the world did you get him to—"

"Tell you later."

"I'll be thinking."

The cocoa was sweet and thick and chocolatey, and the fruitcake tasted like all the Christmases Beth could remember. It would have been nice just to sit there and look at the radiant tree and not worry about Pete Abel. But she couldn't.

"Come on," she said to Trace, enjoying the unusual sensation of having him in her power, to do what she told him. "Come on, Margaret. Mama, we're going to try what you said—eliminating boys. Trace is going to phone them for me, because they might tell another boy easier than they would a girl."

"Well, isn't that nice of Trace!" Mama said. She didn't mean to sound surprised, Beth knew, but her tone let on that she could hardly believe that Trace was going to help Beth—and that Beth was going to let him.

"Sure is," Beth said, winking at Maggie. Maggie giggled. Trace scowled.

"All right, let's get it over with," he growled. Beth could see Mama and Champ looking at each other and thinking, Maybe they're going to be friends, after all.

I would if he would, Beth thought.

Mama said, "Well, if you all will excuse me, I have a few more presents to wrap, up in my room."

"Can we put the presents under the tree tonight? It'll look more Christmasy," Maggie said. She had hers all wrapped, and they looked so beautiful that she was dying to bring them out and let everybody guess what was in them. She thought she had it fixed so they'd never guess—Beth was the only one in on the secret. Maggie had put the little presents in big boxes, and whenever she could she had squeezed big things into smaller boxes than they should have gone in. It was going to be great to see how surprised everybody would be when they opened the presents. Beth sort of wished she had thought of it first. Hers were all wrapped too and looked gay, but anybody smart could guess what they were, she suspected.

"Perhaps just before we go to bed," Mama promised Maggie.

"Maybe we shouldn't," Beth said. "The Goofy Ornament-Grabber might come back. Maybe we'd better keep them hidden."

"We can lock the doors and windows from inside

when we go to bed," Maggie argued. "And some of us will be here tomorrow until Champ gets the keys made, and then when we all go out we can leave the doors locked. I want to put my presents under the tree tonight."

"The Establishment thinks we'd better take a vote," Mama said. "All in favor of putting the presents under the tree tonight at bedtime, say 'Aye.' "

Everybody said "Aye" except Pip—who said "Me!"—and Trace, who didn't vote. He was already on his way to the hall to telephone when Maggie started talking about the presents, and he didn't seem to care.

"Come on if you're coming," he called grumpily. "I can't wait all night. I've got something else to do."

"You've still got to wrap your presents, Trace?" Maggie asked. "Want me to help you? Girls can wrap better than boys. I mean—" she added hastily, "after you've got mine done, of course, so I won't see it."

"I'm not giving any presents," Trace said. "And I hope nobody gives me any."

"Oh, Trace! You can't be like that at Christmas—" Maggie screwed up her face the way she did when she was really upset.

Beth said, "What did you do with your Christmas money, then? The five dollars they gave each of us besides our allowance to buy our presents with? Maggie and I made some of our presents, though—just because it's fun to make things for Christmas. But we bought some too and helped Pip buy hers. And Mama helped her buy things for us. What did you—"

"None of your business," Trace said rudely. "Do you or don't you want me to do what I promised? Because in about one minute I'm going upstairs."

"All right," Beth said, handing him a list she'd been making. "Call up these guys and see if they'll tell you. They all have light hair. I'll think of some others."

"I'll help Pip take her bath," Maggie said. "I already helped her wrap her presents, all except mine. She did that one all by herself, didn't you, Pip?"

A little later, Beth had to report to Mama that eliminating boys worked out too well—Trace had eliminated all of them. She knocked on the door and called, "Have you finished wrapping mine, Mama? Can I come in?"

Mama answered, "Yes, come on in, Beth." She looked very Christmasy in her green slacks and sweater, Beth thought, sitting on the red rug in her room, surrounded by Christmas papers and ribbons and boxes. A pile of pretty packages was stacked up beside her. "I'm nearly through. Where are the others?"

"Pip and Maggie are still taking a bath, Trace went to his room, and Champ is making himself a sandwich." Beth dropped to her knees and sat back on her heels beside Mama. "Mama, would you believe it, some of those boys said they couldn't even remember where they were last night? Some of them thought it was a joke, and said, You're putting me on! And a few of them said right off where they were. But nobody sounded the least bit like he might be the one who took our Christmas tree things. Of course I didn't really think it could have been any of our friends though. It must have been some boy we don't even know."

"He'd have to be one who doesn't go to school," Mama said thoughtfully, "or you'd know him. At least by sight. But of course, boys don't have to go to school after they're sixteen. If they want to they can drop out and get a job at the mill. You wouldn't think though that a boy like that would be bothering about stealing Christmas tree ornaments."

"It just doesn't make any sense at all," Beth said, discouraged. "Most anybody could buy all the Christmas tree ornaments he needed."

"Not everybody has five dollars for Christmas money, Beth," Mama said gently. "Some folks need all they can scrape together for food and rent and clothes. Suppose somebody had a little brother or two or three, and had to get each one a toy or two, and diun't have any money left for ornaments, though he could cut a tree in the woods? It has to be a case like that."

"If only," Beth said disconsolately, "I hadn't been so quick to jump to conclusions, like you say, Mama! I'm always putting my foot in it that way. Now, even if I do find out who did it and clear Pete, I'll get somebody else in trouble. And if it was for a poor kid's Christmas, I don't want to—"

"Well, you aren't very likely to find out," Mama said realistically. "And if you did, all we'd have to do would be to clear Pete with Chief Steadman. We wouldn't have to make any big case out of it."

Beth sighed. "I've only got one more day. Mama, what'll I do if I can't clear Pete by tomorrow? Do you think maybe I should give him the rest of my Christmas money? Or a present? I've got about half the money left, because I made some of my presents, you know, instead of buying them. I was going to spend the rest of it tomorrow, getting a few last-minute store-bought things for everybody I made something for, in case they don't like homemade presents. I know Jane and Connie and Pip and Maggie'll love theirs though. I made them the cutest hair-ribbon trees. I saw them in a teen magazine. You spray crab-apple branches gold and anchor each one in a little pot with clay and bobby-pin a hair bow to each thorn. I had to buy the gold and the bows, of course. They'll love them! I wish they wore hair ribbons. They might start wearing them though. But do you think I ought to give Pete Abel something for Christmas, to kind of make up for—"

"No, honey. I don't think that's a good reason for giving a Christmas present, do you?"

"I guess not. You shouldn't try to give somebody

something just to make yourself feel better about what you did wrong. But how am I going to make it up to him then? It looks like I've just got to find out who really did it," she concluded.

Mama tried to help her think about Christmas instead. "Look what I've got for Trace," she confided. "It's the most expensive turtle-neck sweater I ever saw —he's just got to like it! Isn't it a lovely blue? He seems to like blue best."

"He won't like it," Beth predicted. "He'll keep right on wearing that old thing with the sleeves that are too short, even if this new one is the exact same color of blue. Mama, won't he ever get over being so bullheaded about things like that? Doesn't it make you mad when he won't wear the nice things you buy him and won't even let you touch the things he had when he came here? He even washes his own clothes!"

"That I can bear," Mama said, laughing a little. "It's a help, really. A boy can put a load of clothes in the washer as well as a girl can, you know. And you do yours and Maggie's and Pip's. It's a job I'm glad to turn over to any competent child who wants to do his own."

Beth sniffed. "Well, if he's going to keep on wearing only the clothes his own mother bought for him, she should've bought permanent-press things. He can't iron worth a darn. He can do handkerchiefs all right, I guess—even Pip could do that—but he looks awful in the shirts he irons. I offered to iron one for him one day, but he wouldn't let me touch it."

"Poor Trace—he's so mixed up about the way he loved his mother. And she must have thought she was buying bargains," Mama said, "but they weren't, really. Phyllis seems to have had a thing about going to sales and buying stuff just because it was cheap. The things didn't fit Trace to begin with. I've managed to get rid of most of the 'bargains' she bought for Champ and Pip while she and Champ were married. And some day I'm going to get up enough nerve to collect all of Trace's old clothes and donate them to the Salvation Army."

"Why don't we do it now?" Beth said. "He's got plenty of new things to wear, and he'll be getting more for Christmas. Some poor kid who's smaller than Trace might like his stuff, and it would be a good idea to put it in the box at the church before they finish up the Christmas baskets tomorrow, in case they know somebody who doesn't have any warm clothes to wear."

"That makes sense," Mama agreed, "only Trace would be so mad at me, he'd never forgive me. He still loves his own mother, you see, and that would just make it worse. Especially at Christmas, I don't want to upset him. Come on, help me carry these downstairs; then you can tell Maggie it's O.K. to bring hers and Pip's to put under the tree. You want to bring yours down too, I suppose?"

"Sure," Beth said. "But I'm afraid they'll guess what those hair-ribbon trees are. They were kind of crazy things to wrap, and the thorns stick out of the holly paper. Don't you suppose everybody will know what they are?"

Mama laughed, and loaded Beth's arms with packages, gathering up the rest herself. "No, Beth, I don't really think they will. It's not a very ordinary sort of present, you know, that a person gets every day. Not like a tie or a pair of socks."

Beth smiled too as they started down the stairs. "I guess you're right, Mama. Hardly anybody ever gets a hair-ribbon tree made out of gold crab-apple branches for Christmas."

"What did you make for Trace?"

"I didn't dare make anything for him. I bought his present. I didn't think he'd like a homemade one. I bought him a record. I found a Donovan single in the seventy-seven-cent ones, and it was one he didn't have! Wasn't that lucky?"

Just as they reached the foot of the stairs, Maggie came bolting out of the living room, calling excitedly, "Elizabeth! Elizabeth!" before she saw them coming down. Little Dog nearly tripped her up, running too and barking.

"Well, what's the matter, Margaret?" Beth almost dropped the packages. "Don't tell me he's done it again! No, he couldn't have—" she gasped. "You don't mean the new ornaments are gone too?"

"No," Maggie said. "Come on! It's not that; he didn't take the new ornaments this time. But, Beth, he brought back your angel! It's right there on top of the tree! Instead of that pointed thing!"

Margaret Finds
Another Clue

"Well, that was a wish that came true fast!" Beth said after she had unceremoniously dumped Mama's packages under the tree and stood looking up fondly at her angel.

"What do you mean?" Maggie was back under the tree where she was arranging her packages and Pip's. She hadn't waited for official permission to bring them down. After all, it was just before bedtime, and that was when Mama had said to bring them.

"I wished on the first star I saw tonight, when I went over to Mr. Smith's. I wished I'd get my angel back."

"Well, I wish you'd wished it would snow too. Since your wish was going to come true."

"That would've been too much," Beth said realistically. "You know it only snows once or twice in a winter, and hardly ever at Christmas. I remember when it snowed once on New Year's day, though."

"It's very mysterious about that angel coming back," Mama said, frowning. "Of course the front door wasn't

locked—nor the back one, for that matter. But Champ
was in the kitchen. None of us was at the front of the
house for a while—I guess we were all upstairs—so
somebody could have slipped in, all right. Fine watch-
dog we've got; Little Dog didn't say a word."

"He was asleep." Maggie defended him, reaching
over to pat him. His tail wagged, but his eyes stayed
closed.

"Well, I'm not going to ask any questions," Beth
said, "as long as I've got my angel back."

"Well, I am," Champ said. He had come running
when he heard Maggie yell and so had Trace. Pip, who
had come down with Maggie after her bath to bring their
presents, looked sweet in her pink nightie and robe.
Champ picked her up and hugged her hard while he
went on talking. "We aren't safe around here if somebody's getting in any time he wants to. It's got to stop."

"He might kidnap Pip next," Maggie said.

"Hush, Maggie, do!" Mama said. "Nobody's going
to kidnap Pip."

"That was what Champ was thinking," Maggie said
defensively. It was too, Beth knew.

"Well, I'm fastening all the windows and putting the
chains on the doors, right now," Champ said. "You
help me, Trace. Every window." He put Pip down and
went to fix the back door. Beth picked the child up.

"She's so sweet, anybody'd want to kidnap her," she
mumbled, nuzzling Pip's neck until the child squealed

and giggled. "But we won't let 'em, will we, Pip?"

"Santa Claus come?" Pip asked.

"Hey, that's an idea—maybe it was Santa who brought back my angel! But no, he's not coming until tomorrow night, Pip. Christmas Eve is when he comes, remember?"

"He'll bring my talking doll," Pip said confidently.

"What're you going to name it, Pip? If you get it?" Maggie grabbed her away from Beth and tumbled her on the sofa.

Pip thought for a while and then out of the past she brought a name she must have heard and dimly remembered.

"Phyllis." Her smile was triumphant.

Trace whirled around from the window he was locking, and strode over and knelt on one knee in front of Pip, grabbing her by the shoulders. "No, Pip," he said sternly. "Not that name. Name it—name it Betty or Susie or Janie. You hear?"

"Phyllis," Pip said sweetly.

"Aw, Trace, why don't you let her name it what she wants to?" Maggie said. Beth wondered if Maggie remembered whose name it was.

"She'd better not let me hear her call it that." Trace scowled at Pip and gave her a little shake. Pip began to cry.

"Never mind," Mama said soothingly to Trace. "She'll forget it." He didn't even glance at Mama; he went back to locking the windows. His back looked so unhappy that Beth felt sorry for him.

"Come on, Pip," she said. "Go to bed now and I'll tuck you in. You can name your new doll—if you get one—after me and Maggie. How about Margaret Elizabeth? Can you say that?"

"Maggie Beth," Pip said delightedly.

"That's a real good name," Maggie said. "Night, Pip."

"The rest of us had better get to bed too," Mama said. "Tomorrow's going to be a busy day."

"Wait till I put my things under the tree," Beth said.

"You can't guess what I've got for you," Maggie said to her.

Beth picked up the big box and shook it.

"Don't shake it too hard," Maggie warned.

"No, I can't guess," Beth said. "But it's so big, I know it's something little inside! Don't you dare touch the one I've got for you." She ran upstairs and hurried back with her arms full of well-dressed packages.

"Mine looks real interesting," Maggie said, reading her name on a card. "And I want to take a look at Mama's presents for us."

"They're from me and Champ together, of course," Mama said. "He can't wrap packages, he says."

"I've still got a little shopping to do tomorrow," Beth remembered.

"I've got some of my Christmas money left too,"

Maggie said. "Can we go together, Beth? I won't look if you want to buy me something."

"Sure," Beth said. "Good night, everybody." She looked up at her angel and said good night to it in her mind. She just knew she wouldn't sleep a wink, for puzzling over how it had disappeared and then had come back.

But she did.

Next morning Champ, who was taking Christmas Eve off and had given the mill a holiday too, got the lock man, Mr. Herman, to come soon after breakfast because it was an emergency. Mr. Herman was really the plumber, but he could fix electric things and locks too. He said he couldn't see how anybody could be so mean as to steal ornaments off somebody's Christmas tree.

He decided the best thing to do was to change the lock and then make duplicate keys to the new one. Pretty soon everybody except Pip had a shiny new key, tied to a Christmas ribbon until The Establishment could buy key rings for them all. Maggie wore hers around her neck. That was O.K. for a ten-year-old, Beth thought, but she tucked hers in her coin purse.

"Now," said Champ, "whenever we're all going out, the last one to leave locks the doors. O.K.?"

"O.K." Just to think about it made Beth feel more secure about her angel. She wondered if maybe they had better alert Jane and Beverly Ann and all the neighbors to start locking their doors too. At least until after Christmas. The Goofy Ornament-Grabber might strike again!

"Now who wants to ride with me to the shopping center this morning?" Champ asked.

"Maggie and I do," Beth said. She knew she ought to be doing something about clearing Pete Abel, but she couldn't think of anything helpful she could possibly do except maybe to talk to Chief Steadman and see if he would try to find some fingerprints or something on the angel. Maybe even if he couldn't tell whose fingerprints they were, he might be able to tell that they weren't Pete's. And that would clear Pete. Of course, if there were no fingerprints at all—which frequently was the case in the mystery stories she read—that would mean the culprit wore gloves. Real criminals nearly always wore gloves. Pete Abel probably didn't own any gloves, so that might be something that would help clear him too.

"Champ," she said as he started the car, "do you suppose Chief Steadman has some of that powder stuff detectives use to find fingerprints on things that criminals have handled? Like my angel? And the stuff to take fingerprints—like maybe Pete Abel's—and compare them?"

"I seriously doubt that Chief Steadman ever had to fingerprint a criminal," Champ said. "You know there aren't very many criminals in Pleasant Grove, Beth."

"That blows it then," Beth said disconsolately. "I thought maybe we could clear Pete that way, and find out who really took the stuff. Like if the criminal's fingerprints were on record in the F.B.I. files or something."

"Not likely," Champ said solemnly. "He probably doesn't ever cross a state line when he steals Christmas tree ornaments, so it wouldn't be a Federal crime."

"Look!" Maggie said. They had already gone by Jane's house and now they were passing some thick woods. Beth saw somebody move in the underbrush.

"I saw him!" Maggie said. "Just as he crawled under the barbed wire. It's Pete Abel, and he's got a gun!"

"Probably trying to shoot some squirrels for their Christmas dinner," Champ said mildly. "Or rabbits,

maybe. No harm in that. If Trace ever showed any interest in hunting, I'd get him a gun and take him sometimes."

"But don't you see, Champ?" Maggie pointed out. "There's a sign that says *Posted. No Hunting.*"

Beth said excitedly, "I'll bet that's where Trace saw him the night of the robbery! Coming out of the woods where there was a *No Hunting* sign, with a gun and a lot of squirrels or rabbits or birds. So naturally he'd be in trouble if Trace told—"

"Could be you're right," Champ said, "though I know Mr. Julius owns these woods, and I don't think he'd mind if a boy hunted a few squirrels. Anyway, how would Trace have got out here, to happen to see Pete that late? It was nearly dark. And Trace doesn't ever go hunting, you know."

"Beats me," Maggie said. "But except for that, Champ, it fits perfectly!"

"When we get back I'll tell Trace we know his secret," Beth said confidently. "And maybe he'll be surprised into admitting we're right. Then we could tell Chief Steadman and he'd—what's that word—absolve Pete from suspicion."

"Pete'd be out of the frying pan, into the fire, though," Maggie said, shaking her head. "He'd still be in trouble." Then she giggled. "He'd look funny, jumping out of a frying pan, wouldn't he?"

"Aw, I bet Champ's right—Mr. Julius wouldn't

care if Pete hunted on his land. He wouldn't do anything to him. Specially at Christmas."

But when they had spent all their money at the shopping center, and Champ had bought them each a hot
dog and a drink, and they had shaken hands with the
department stores' Santa Clauses (even though girls
their age didn't tell pretend Santas what they wanted
for Christmas) and had looked in all the store windows and had sprayed perfume on themselves from all
the atomizers on the cosmetics counters in the stores
and had come home carrying gay, red-and-green sacks
containing the things they'd bought, Trace wouldn't
admit at all that he'd seen Pete Abel hunting on posted
land.

"No," he said flatly. "I didn't see him there."

"Then where *did* you see him?" Beth demanded.
"Look, Trace, get me off the hook, will you? It would
be the best Christmas present you could give me, and it
wouldn't cost a thing."

"I told you I'm not giving any Christmas presents,
and I don't want any."

"Well, you could tell me what I need to know to
make Pete's alibi sound reasonable to Chief Steadman.
You believe in peace-on-earth-good-will-to-men, don't
you?"

"I told you I know he didn't do it. That ought to be
enough."

"You're hopeless. I think maybe it would be a good

idea to put switches in your stocking, like Champ said they do in Germany for kids who won't cooperate."

"Who cares what you think?"

Maggie said, "Oh, no, Beth—"

But just to tease him, after lunch Beth went out to the wooded vacant lot at the back of their house and began to break off some long slender branches for switches. Maggie kept trying to discourage her, but Beth thought it would be a good joke on Trace. Champ had told them about Christmas customs in Germany, and this was the one that appealed to her.

Then she heard Maggie say in a different, sort of shook-up tone, "Look here, Beth! Look what I've found. Do you think it's what I think it is? Do you think it's—a clue?"

The Ashes
Behind the Garage

Beth hurried over to where Maggie was staring at the ground.

"It sure is a clue!" she agreed. Maggie had found a small stump, newly sawed, where a pine tree with a trunk about as big around as an orange-juice glass had grown. "I bet this is where the Goofy Ornament-Grabber cut the tree he was going to decorate with our things!"

"So we can tell how big his tree is," Maggie said. "That one over there has a trunk about as big as this one was."

Beth measured with her eyes the tree Maggie pointed out, which was maybe a foot taller than she. "It's not so awfully big," she said doubtfully. " 'Most everybody has a bigger tree than that."

"So if we should see a tree this size in somebody's house," Maggie said, "it would more than likely be the one!"

"Especially if it had that German singing bird on

it," Beth scoffed. "You know we aren't going to see it in anybody's house we know. In fact," she went on thoughtfully, "that bit itself might be a clue. The Goofy Ornament-Grabber would have to live somewhere else, where we'd never see the tree he decorated with the things he took. Because he wouldn't dare use them where anybody around here could ever see them, would he? Even Chief Steadman ought to believe that Pete Abel would have better sense than that, even if he is against Pete because Pete's done bad things before."

"You're right. Those ornaments would have to be used on a tree nobody in Pleasant Grove was ever supposed to see."

"This gets harder and harder to figure out," Beth said dismally. She forgot about the switches and left them where she had dropped them on the ground. They went back to the house.

"Hey, Mama!" Maggie said when they went in the kitchen. "We found the stump where the Goofy Ornament-Grabber cut the tree he was going to put our ornaments on!"

Mama said, "Where in the world—"

"In the lot behind our yard. I guess it was real handy."

"But wait a minute!" Beth said. "When I saw him that night he was running off with the stuff—and he didn't have any tree. So he would've had to cut it either before or after the time he stole the ornaments. If he had cut it before, that would mean he had it all planned ahead. So why cut a tree in this particular lot? There are lots of trees out in the woods."

Maggie said, "Maybe he didn't have a car. Maybe he didn't even have a bicycle."

"That's right. Well, I don't suppose there are any fingerprints on that stump, even if Chief Steadman happened to have a fingerprinting kit."

"They were giving away a fingerprinting kit with cereal box tops last summer," Maggie said. "We should've ordered one. We could give it to Chief Steadman for a Christmas present." She giggled.

Mama said, "Have you forgotten about making the Christmas cookies this afternoon? The dough for the gingerbread men is cooling in the refrigerator, and I've got the raisins and the red and green sugar and everything else for the sugar cookies. Beth, you find the Christmas cooky cutters, and Maggie, you go and get Pip and tell Trace."

"Trace will say he dosn't like to make Christmas cookies," Beth predicted. "There hasn't been a single thing yet about Christmas that Trace likes."

Sure enough, Maggie came back with Pip—who was bubbling with excitement at the idea of really making a gingerbread man and a Christmas tree out of cooky dough the way Maggie had told her she could—but Trace had said he was going to stay in his room and he didn't want anything to do with Christmas cookies, not even to eat them.

"And that's not normal," Maggie said to Mama,

screwing up her face anxiously. "Trace must be sick. Don't you think you had better take his temperature, Mama?"

"Not right now," Mama said. "No, Maggie, I don't think he's sick—not the way you could tell by taking his temperature, anyhow. He's emotionally upset by Christmas without his own mother, that's all. He wants her back and he hasn't adjusted yet."

"Well, he ought to realize he can't ever have her back," Beth said, feeling sad in spite of the red and green sugar and the cooky dough waiting. "So he'll just have to get along the same way Maggie and I are trying to do without Daddy."

"It's not quite the same," Mama said. "If she were dead, you see, it would be easier to accept the fact."

"Mama! What do you mean, *if* she were dead? Trace's mother—she *is* dead—he said—"

Mama was looking at her the way she did when she was trying to decide whether Beth was old enough. Only this time it wasn't about the pale-pink lipstick and the panty-hose.

She said at last, after making sure Pip was absorbed in sorting out the cooky cutters and not paying any attention to the others, "No, she isn't. I thought you knew. They were divorced. Phyllis isn't dead. She lives in Oklahoma with her sister, Trace's Aunt Jo."

"Trace said she was dead. Lots of times." Beth couldn't understand it. Maggie looked puzzled too.

"That's—well, it's strange," Mama said, "but I think maybe I know why. He couldn't accept the fact that his father had to divorce his mother, you see, because Trace loves her so much. He was too young to understand all the reasons why Champ thought it was best for Phyllis not to live with them any more. You're too young too—you'll understand some day. But Trace sensed that it was something people would call disgraceful. So he felt he would rather she'd be dead. So he just said she was dead and tried to believe it and tried to make everybody else believe it. He made his father promise not ever to talk about her. I guess that's why we've never discussed her, so that you never happened to hear it was a divorce, and naturally believed what Trace said about her being dead."

"That's why he wouldn't let Pip name the doll Phyllis," Maggie said thoughtfully. "He really does wish she was dead and he'd never have to hear of her again."

"Except," Beth said, "he still hangs onto everything he has that she bought for him."

"That's the way it is sometimes," Mama said gently. "Love and hate are so close together you can't always tell them apart. Trace still loves his mother more than he knows, even if he can't bear to think about her or hear her name. He doesn't really understand about the divorce yet, nor why it had to be. But some day he'll know Champ was right to give him and Pip a new, normal home, far away from Phyllis. She kept them all stirred up emotionally all the time—an atmosphere that wasn't good for children to grow up in. Trace is having a very hard time right now adjusting to the whole thing. Let's all be very gentle with him and not bother him about it, and maybe he'll be better by next Christmas. Come on now, who wants to start with gingerbread men, and who wants the sugar-cooky dough? Pip, honey, you can make your cookies, but as soon as they're done you have to take your nap, O.K.?"

"O.K.," Pip said angelically. First she let Maggie rub flour on her chubby hands; then she pushed the rolling pin forward and sideways, the way Beth showed her; then she pressed the cooky cutter hard into the dough.

"Isn't she cute?" Beth whispered. "And her gingerbread man's not bad, either. See, Pip, you can put raisins on his coat for buttons and give him currants for eyes and a smile cut out of a candied cherry. Then we'll put him on the cooky sheet to bake."

"See, like mine," Maggie said. "I'll do a Santa next."

"I'll start on a Christmas tree," Beth said. "I'll divide the sugar-cooky dough and put green coloring in some."

They worked happily for an hour or so, and the fragrant smell of baking cookies filled the house.

"I bet old Trace wishes he hadn't said he didn't want any, if he can smell them up there in his room," Beth said, nibbling on a warm piece of a star that had broken when she tried to slide it off the cooky sheet too soon. She gave Pip the other piece. "Stars taste very good," she told her.

"Leave some for Santa?" Pip said. Maggie had told her that she was supposed to leave a plate of cookies and a glass of milk in front of the fireplace where Santa would be sure to see them when he came down the chimney. "Santa like stars?"

"Maybe he'd like the reindeer ones better," Maggie said. "Little Dog likes broken reindeer bits." She gave him one and he snapped it up, tail wagging. "You can pick out the prettiest whole ones, Pip, from all our plates. You can have my gingerbread man for Santa if you like," she offered generously. Each girl had a large holly-design tray on which to display her own special cookies, to offer her friends when they came by next day to compare what everybody had got for Christmas.

"Now Pip goes upstairs to take her nap," Mama said. "Take one cooky with you if you like, honey. Beth, will you tuck her in?"

"C'mon, Pip, I'll race you," Beth said.

She came back to report that Pip was in bed, but it wasn't very likely she could go to sleep. "Have you forgotten, Mama, how exciting it was the day before Christmas, waiting for Santa Claus? I never could get to sleep at night—much less take a nap."

"I remember," Mama said. "I remember one Christmas Eve when you two were awake until four in the morning." Maggie and Beth giggled.

"I actually used to hear reindeer hoofs and jingle bells on the roof," Maggie said. "I really actually thought I did."

"Imagination is wonderful," Mama agreed. "I hope Pip has plenty of imagination too."

"And Mama," Beth said solemnly, "it really is kind of true, what you told us. That Santa Claus really does bring the presents as long as you believe he does. Whatever you truly believe is so. It was so wonderful, believing in Santa! When you stop believing in him, then of course, parents have to give you the presents. You and Daddy always gave us a present too though, even when Santa brought the toys. That was pretty clever of you."

"I think it's really more fun," Maggie said, "to be giving presents too, like we do now. I just love to wrap presents. And that reminds me, Beth, we haven't wrapped the things we bought this morning."

"First," Mama said, "clean up all this mess."

"It's a pretty nice mess," Maggie said, running a finger around the bowl and licking off the green cooky dough and then scraping out some red icing from another bowl. "Have some, Beth?"

"We'll clean up as soon as we lick the bowls, Mama," Beth promised.

"We should've let Pip lick some too," Maggie said. "And if old Trace would act decent about Christmas, we'd give him a few licks."

"Let's not even think about Trace," Beth said. "He

spoils my Christmas. And I still haven't done anything about Pete Abel. Mama, would it be all right if I were to take some of my best cookies over to Pete and his sister? I know that wouldn't be as good as finding out who really stole the things, but it might—well, it might be good-will-to-men. It's not like that silly idea I had about money or a Christmas present. Cookies aren't a present. And tonight after the cantata at the church when Mr. Fred takes all the Sunday-school kids to sing carols at everybody's house, we might get them to go over there and sing 'We Wish You a Merry Christmas.' Maybe Pete and Goldie wouldn't feel quite so—so unfriendly if we did that."

"Of course, sing the carols for them," Mama said. "And I suppose it would be all right to take them some cookies. Champ and I have to go a few places this afternoon, and we may not be back until late, but we'll be here in plenty of time for a late supper and the Christmas singing at the church. You'll be home well before dark, won't you? I guess Trace will look after Pip."

"Sure," Beth said. "But let's wrap the other presents first, huh, Maggie?"

It took only a little while. Beth finished first and told Maggie she was going down to pack cookies for the Abels in the red tin box the fruitcake had come in.

"You can take some of my nicest ones too," Maggie said.

"Thanks, Margaret. But you needn't. After all, this is my problem, trying to make up for something I did."

"But I want to help," Maggie said earnestly. "I always feel very generous around Christmas time. So let me help—Elizabeth?"

"Well, O.K. I'll tell them the cookies are from both of us then. I'll put both names on the card."

Beth fixed the box with tissue paper inside and red cellophane between the layers of cookies. She tied a wide green ribbon around the box, fastening it with cellophane tape where it slipped on the round edges, and made a big bow in the middle. It was just about the prettiest package she had done. But she thought it needed something more. There were some red Nandina berries on a bush behind the garage. I'll get some sprigs of boxwood, she thought, and a spray of the red berries and put them in the center of that green bow.

She already had gathered the boxwood and the berries, and had squinted at the massing gray clouds and wished they meant snow, when she saw something odd on the ground behind the garage. She poked at it for a minute with growing excitement, and then ran to call

Maggie. It looked like a little pile of ashes where something had been burned. She thought, We missed all sorts of clues at first by not looking around outside the house.

"Margaret!" She ran into their room and closed the door, so as not to wake Pip in case she might have gone to sleep after all. She didn't want Pip asking to go with them to take the cookies to the Abels.

"What now?"

"Come with me. It's another clue!"

Little Dog jumped up and followed them.

The Goofy Ornament-Grabber Strikes Again

"You see?" Beth said.

"I don't see a thing except some—is it ashes? Looks like somebody burned something out here behind the garage."

"Look closer," Beth urged. "He was in a hurry, see? Somebody must have been about to catch him after he stole it from the house. Like if we were about to take out the garbage. He had to get rid of it so it wouldn't be found on him if he was caught. And he didn't have time to wait and check to see if it had all burned. Or maybe he thought it had all burned. Anyhow, it didn't quite. Look, what are those the ashes of?"

"Paper?" Maggie was puzzled.

"Paper, yes—he had to start it burning with paper. But there's a little piece of cloth left that for some reason didn't burn. Margaret," she said solemnly, "it's got to be that missing handkerchief!" She poked at the ashes and pointed out the bits of charred white cloth that had escaped the flames. "You do see?" she urged.

"Yes," Maggie said. "You're right. It could be the handkerchief all right. Even if it's not the corner with the *Z* on it."

"He probably started with that corner, so it would be sure to burn up all right." Beth gathered up the ashes, being very careful with the bits of cloth to keep them from disintegrating, and cupped them in her hand until she could get inside and find a box to put them in. "If Chief Steadman was a book detective," she said, "he could reconstruct something from these ashes. But it doesn't really matter. We know it was the handkerchief. What we don't know is who dropped it in the first place and then stole it out of my drawer and burned it to keep it from being a clue."

"Mama and Champ have already gone visiting," Maggie said. "You want to ask Trace what he thinks?"

"No. I wouldn't ask old Trace anything. Let's put the ashes away and go on over to the Abels' with the cookies."

"Well, we've got to tell him we're going, so he can look after Pip."

They peeped in Pip's room and told Trace that she had finally gone to sleep. Trace muttered, "O.K."

Little Dog wanted to go too, so they took him along. "We'll have to hurry to get back before dark, like Mama said." Maggie looked worried. "You think it's already getting dark, or are those snow clouds making everything gray?" she asked hopefully.

"Not a chance," Beth said. "We've never had a white Christmas yet."

They took a short cut past Ginny's grandmother's house, but didn't see anybody. "It's so cold everybody's indoors," Maggie said. She glanced over toward Trace's stark old tower, at the edge of the field between the house and the railroad track.

Beth noticed and said, "Well, at least he's not up there today."

They went down under the railroad bridge and walked along by the railroad, taking the short cut, not going around through town this time because they were in a hurry—though when they were going anywhere and had the time, they always took the main street detour so they could look in the store windows. This time it was different. It would be scary to be out at the Abels' even at twilight; and dark came very early in December.

"Maybe we'll get to see inside their place this time," Maggie said hopefully.

"Maybe we oughtn't to go in," Beth said. She wouldn't give Trace credit, but maybe he'd had a point there, when he warned them. "I kind of wish we could just leave the box by their door and not even see them. Because I promised Pete I'd find out who really did it, and I haven't. So I can't do what I wanted to and clear him before Christmas."

"Well, nothing bad has happened to him about it

anyhow," Maggie said. "I expect Chief Steadman forgot about it because it's Christmas time."

"I wish I could forget about it," Beth said. "It's awful to have a conscience, Maggie. Let's hurry; it's getting darker every minute."

As they left the populated part of town and started down the unpaved road, Maggie said nervously, "I think—I saw somebody in those trees. I think we're being followed!"

"Oh, no, Maggie!" But Little Dog barked and growled. And they hurried, almost running, toward the railroad car where they saw light behind the windows.

Their fright was a good reason to knock, after all. Beth decided they should say "Merry Christmas," even if it might sound sort of crazy coming from her before she had made everything all right for Pete, and after he had kind of threatened to do something to her if she didn't.

It was Pete's big sister Goldie who opened the door, and she said, "Come in," though not very enthusiastically. Nobody else was at home. Maggie looked, big-eyed, at the railroad car's housekeeping arrangements, while Beth explained about the cookies. There was an iron stove with a fire in it and a pot and a kettle on top. Something was cooking that smelled good. Maggie wondered if a cardboard kind of partition at the back of the car hid a bed and maybe a bathroom. There were two cots covered with patchwork quilts against the long side of the car. There were a small table and a bench and two stools, and faded pink curtains hung over the windows that weren't broken. Maggie wished she had had a railroad car to make a playhouse in, when she was little. It would have been almost as good as the old tower.

The place was nice and clean, and Goldie even had some red berries and pine twigs in a glass on the table. But she didn't have a Christmas tree. Maggie guessed it was because there weren't any small kids—but she hoped she'd never get too big to want a Christmas tree.

Beth was explaining, "I couldn't exactly find out who it was that took the things instead of Pete. Not yet, but I will. But I thought maybe he'd be willing to believe I'm sorry, if I brought some of the Christmas cookies we made. Do you think he might?" she appealed to Goldie.

"I don't know," Goldie said, accepting the box. "Thanks, though. But Pete is pretty mad about the whole thing. You can't blame him, can you? When a kid has been trying to do right and live down some of the bad things he did when he was younger, and then gets jumped on for something he didn't do—well, it makes everything seem pretty useless."

"I know," Beth said earnestly. "That's why I want so much to find out who really did it. It's even worse, at Christmas. I feel terrible about it. Would you—could you, Goldie—try to explain to him that I'm sorry, and I'm trying as hard as I can to get it straightened out?"

"I'll try," Goldie said. "But like I said, he's pretty mad at you. Don't get scared if you catch him hanging around your house or following you. I don't think he'd do anything to hurt you; he's just got some kind of fool idea that he might see whoever it really was, trying something else, if he hangs around your place."

"Maybe that was Pete we thought was following us when we came down your road," Maggie said.

"I'll bet it was. He's out somewhere." Goldie went over to the stove and took the pot lid off and stirred the food with a big spoon.

"What are you cooking?" Maggie asked. "It smells good."

"Rabbit stew. Pete went hunting."

"We saw him—this morning. When Champ was driving us to the shopping center."

Goldie looked as if she wished she had said it was lamb stew she had bought at the supermarket. "You won't—"

"No, of course we won't tell. But Champ thinks Mr. Julius wouldn't care, even though his woods are posted."

"Well, don't tell, anyhow."

"We think that's why Trace won't say where Pete was when our stuff was stolen. Trace might have seen him hunting where he oughtn't to have been."

The platform door was pushed open then, and Pete came in. The girls said Hello, and Beth added bravely, in spite of his glum look, "Merry Christmas, Pete. We made Christmas cookies and brought you and Goldie some."

"Thanks," he said bitterly. He took off his old Army jacket and hung it on a nail in the corner and held his hands over the stove, rubbing them together to warm them.

"Try a gingerbread man," Maggie urged. "They're real good."

Pete grunted. Goldie took the ribbon carefully off the box and opened it. "They're pretty," she said. "Come on, Pete, forget it. Eat some of the cookies they brought. It's Christmas."

"Fine Christmas for me." But he took a green-sugared Christmas tree and ate it slowly, and Beth took heart. Maybe he'd forgive her after all.

Maggie said, "Were you following us when we came over here? Somebody was, and it scared us. It even scared Little Dog." He was close to her feet, and wagged his tail when she mentioned his name. She thought, Little Dog's polite, anyway. He doesn't growl at Pete in his own house.

"Might've been me," Pete said. "Might not."

Beth had an idea. "Say! Goldie told us you've been watching around our house—and I don't blame you a bit—trying to see if the Goofy Ornament-Grabber tried it again. Well, he did. Last night. Were you out there? Did you see anybody sneak in?"

"You mean something else is missing?"

"Well, he stole some food—and the handkerchief that was the clue to the ornaments. But that was probably in the afternoon. Last night, between, oh, about nine and ten o'clock, somebody slipped in when we were all upstairs, except Champ, our stepfather. He was in the kitchen. But whoever it was didn't steal anything that time. He brought back my angel and put it right where it was, on top of the tree! Did you—were you there? Did you see anybody at all around our house who looked suspicious?"

Pete frowned. "That's funny," he said. "Real strange. I was watching your house between nine and ten o'clock. Earlier than that too. I saw you go out to Smith's, and Trace go out before you did. And I saw you both come back. But that was before nine. I was hiding across the street behind Miss Carrie's camellia bushes and I heard her clock strike nine. Between nine and ten o'clock nobody went near your house. Nobody," he repeated with emphasis.

Beth stared at him, and Maggie screwed up her face.

"You're sure?" Beth said. "Positive? Because— that's impossible. It makes the whole thing more of a mystery than ever."

"Not anybody at all," Pete said. "I wouldn't kid you. I'd have seen if anybody went in or out."

Maggie said, "The Goofy Ornament-Grabber has got to be invisible. Maybe he put fern seed in his shoes."

"You don't believe stuff like that, do you?" Pete was scornful. "Ferns don't have seeds."

"That's why it could be true, don't you see?" Maggie tried to explain it to him. "Because if nobody ever saw any seeds on ferns, then if you could put fern seeds in your shoes you really might become invisible. Nobody knows that you wouldn't, because nobody could ever check it out. See?"

"Daddy used to say nothing is impossible," Beth said. "He said if television is possible, anything is possible."

Pete shrugged and turned away. "Well, I'm darn sure nobody went into your house between nine and ten last night."

"It's getting to be more of a mystery all the time." Beth was really puzzled. "But I'll keep trying to solve it, on account of needing to clear you, Pete. Maggie, we've got to go. It's getting darker. Hope you all have a good Christmas," she said, wondering how they could.

"Yes, Merry Christmas," Maggie said. Little Dog wagged his good wishes.

"Merry Christmas," Goldie echoed. "Thanks for the cookies. We'll have some of them for Christmas dinner. We've got a chicken too. Somebody gave it to us," she added hurriedly. Beth realized she didn't want them to think Pete had shot somebody's chicken while he was out hunting.

"Bye." All three girls said it, but Pete didn't say anything. Goldie came to the door with them.

"Look! It's snowing!" Beth said. "It's really snowing!" As they left, Goldie shut the door quickly behind them to keep out the cold wind.

There were only a few flakes falling so far, but it was exciting to think there just might be a white Christmas after all. Little Dog caught the excitement and barked.

"Hurry, Maggie!" Beth said. "Won't it be neat if there's snow tonight when we go out to sing the Christmas carols? We'll look like a Christmas card, with snow on our red caps and mittens."

"I'll bet this will be the first white Christmas Pleasant Grove's ever had," Maggie said happily. "It's cold though, isn't it?"

"Snow's hardly ever hot." They both giggled, half-running across the long field behind Ginny's grandmother's, lifting their faces to feel the soft, cold flakes fall on their cheeks and melt there. Little Dog ran too. The house was dark except for the Christmas lights; the family was probably already at the church getting it ready for the cantata, Beth thought.

"Won't Pip be excited?" Maggie said. "Maybe she hasn't ever seen snow."

Little Dog was sniffing at something on the ground, and Maggie pulled on his leash. "Come on, Little Dog. Mama said to get home before dark, and it's dark

already. But that's because snow came; it's really not
suppertime yet."

Little Dog refused to budge. He kept on sniffing.

"What's he doing?" Beth said impatiently. She bent
over to look. "Why, that no-count cat! It's the collar
you bought for Useless, Maggie. He must have pulled
it off going through a hole in the fence."

"He loves going through wire fences." Maggie
excused him. "That's why I bought a snap-on collar,
you know, so he wouldn't get hung up and choke to
death. Let's have it, I'll take it back to him."

"Imagine old Useless coming way over here," Beth
said.

"Oh, he goes all over. He's the wandering kind.
Remember when Champ saw him having dinner over
at the restaurant that time?" She put the collar in her
coat pocket, and they went on home.

"Why, the front door's not locked!" Beth said.
"That Trace! We told him we were going out, and he
should have put the chain on from inside. If I'd known
he wouldn't, I'd have locked it myself from the outside."

"Boys are just careless," Maggie said. "You can't
trust them to do anything right."

They hurried into the living room to check the tree.
"Well, thank goodness it's all right!" Beth said, seeing
her angel still in place. "Plug in the lights, Maggie.
I'll turn on the outdoor ones. Old Trace could have

done that much, it seems to me. He must still be sulking in his room, if Pip is still asleep. She's not likely to be though."

"Wonder if the back door's locked?" Maggie said. She went back to see, after making the Christmas tree bloom with its soft brilliance.

It was locked, all right, but when she passed through the kitchen she noticed that the refrigerator door was slightly ajar. She looked in. She remembered there had been three full cartons of milk when she poured some for lunch. Now there were only two.

"Elizabeth!" she called. Beth came running. "How many cartons of milk ought to be in here? The refrigerator was open."

"Three," Beth said promptly. "Aren't there three in there?"

"The Goofy Ornament-Grabber is a milk-grabber too," Maggie told her. "Wonder what else is missing?"

Beth's heart nearly stopped beating. Maggie had the same thought at the same time. The house was ominously quiet.

"Pip!"

They raced upstairs, calling, "Pip! Pip! Where are you?"

There wasn't a sound upstairs.

They opened the door to Pip's room. From the tumbled bed, Teddy and Raggedy Ann and Raggedy Andy stared back with their shoe-button eyes.

Pip wasn't there. Pip, they knew in their frightened hearts, wasn't anywhere in the house.

Maggie sobbed, "I told you. I told you Pip would be kidnapped!"

Where
Is Pip?

"Hold it!" Beth said. "Maybe she's not kidnapped. Where's Trace? He was supposed to be looking after her. Probably she's all right. But why would he take her out in this kind of weather, on Christmas Eve? To play in the snow, maybe? But why wouldn't he leave a note to say where they've gone? He knows that's one of The Establishment's rules."

"He's been kidnapped too," Maggie said ominously. "There are whole gangs of kidnappers. I've read about them. They even kidnap grown men sometimes. Well, at least they took some milk for Pip. I'm glad of that."

"They only kidnap grown men if the men are millionaires," Beth said. "And who'd want old Trace?"

"But if Pip and Trace were both kidnapped, that would explain why there's no note. He wouldn't have had a chance to write a note, would he? The kidnappers might not have let him."

"Let's not panic. How do we know there's not a note somewhere?" Beth said. "Let's go down and look everywhere he might have left a note."

They searched everywhere downstairs. No note.

"Well, how about his room? I'll bet he was writing it there when the kidnappers came and snatched them away." Maggie still held to her theory about the kidnappers. Beth wanted to find a note that said where Trace had gone with Pip, and why.

"He'll kill us for searching his room," Beth said. "But this is an emergency. I guess we've got to do it."

"I've always wanted to poke around in his room anyhow," Maggie said. "But Mama said we didn't have any right to if he didn't want us in there. And he sure didn't."

"This is different." Beth opened Trace's door. Everything looked normal. "No sign of a struggle," she said. "Now where would a note be—if he'd written one?"

There was no note on his desk. They looked on the bureau and even inside the drawers. No note. "On his pillow? I once saw a movie where a boy ran away from home and left a note on his pillow," Maggie said.

"Did he take his baby sister with him?" Beth was more worried than she wanted to admit. There was no note on the pillow, nor under it.

"Let's check his closet and see what he wore," Maggie suggested. "They always say on TV what the missing people were wearing."

"We've got to hunt up Mama and Champ and tell them," Beth said.

"Tell them Pip and Trace have been kidnapped,"

Maggie said darkly, opening the closet door. "Except we don't know where to find Mama and Champ. They were going several places for Christmas visits, they said, but they didn't say which."

"There's no time to waste!" Beth said. "Something bad might have happened—" She didn't know what, but she had an apprehensive feeling that she wished she could do something about.

Maggie started checking the clothes hanging in the closet. "His leather jacket is gone." It was the first time she had ever been that close to Trace's things. Inquisitively, she felt in the pockets of the old Army jacket of Champ's that hung next to the empty hanger where the leather coat had been. Nothing there, though.

Beth said excitedly, "Here's something on the floor. It's—"

"A note!" Maggie pounced on it. "He dropped it when he was getting his jacket, more than likely, and was in a hurry and didn't miss it. He must have forgotten that he was planning to leave it where we could see it."

Beth grabbed it and read it out loud. "I'm taking Pip to Ben and Beverly Ann's house to see their Christmas tree," it read.

"That sure is funny." Maggie frowned, trying to figure it out. "Why would he do that? I don't think he's been to Ben's in months. If he ever went. He's not real good friends with anybody." Absent-mindedly she

wiped her hand on her corduroy slacks. Something was clinging to her fingers. Then she looked down at the brown corduroy. "Angel-hair!" she said, puzzled. "I got angel-hair on my hand from Trace's pocket. Why do you suppose—"

"I guess he must have had some angel-hair in his pocket sometime," Beth said, her mind still on Pip's safety. "Look, let's go and call Ben's and ask if they're there."

Ben's mother said No, she hadn't seen anything of

Trace and Pip. They hadn't been at her house at all.

Beth hung up the receiver and sat staring worriedly at Maggie. "They aren't there. They never were."

"Try some others."

Beth called all the little kids Pip played with most often. But nobody had seen Trace and Pip.

"Well," Maggie said, "at least Trace is with her. She ought to be O.K."

"We don't know for sure. If you should happen to be right about a kidnapper, he might have got Pip, and Trace might have followed him to try to rescue her. I think we ought to tell Mama and Champ."

"Who can we call to find them?"

"Well, we don't actually know there's anything wrong. They wouldn't want us to upset everybody on Christmas Eve if Pip is just out somewhere with Trace. Let's call some of Mama and Champ's friends and see if we can find them—but not say why we're hunting for them."

After calling different friends for ten minutes without any luck, Beth said, "I guess maybe we ought to be out looking for Pip and Trace instead. I don't believe it's any use calling anybody else. We're just wasting time. No telling where Mama and Champ are. They probably went to Monroe or Covington to do some last-minute Christmas shopping. And they could have had car trouble or something. The snow's sticking on the ground now. The road might be slick and that might

slow them down. Let's go look for Pip and Trace. They
might be building a snowman somewhere with some
kids. We could ask—if we see anybody on the street—
if they saw them. We could take Little Dog to smell
them out."

"Hey, that's an idea!" Maggie said. "He can track
them. We can give him something they've worn, to
smell, the way they do with bloodhounds."

"Let's get something out of Trace's laundry bag,"
Beth said. They raced back to Trace's room.

"Wouldn't he kill us though!" Maggie dumped out
his laundry bag in the middle of the floor. "There's a
pair of his old too-little pajamas," she said. "Will
they do?"

Beth was staring at something else she saw in the pile
of laundry. In the back of her mind something was beginning to connect with something else tantalizingly.
Angel-hair . . . Army jacket. . . . She almost knew what
it was, and then it eluded her. Some little thing she
ought to remember that would make something about
the mystery clear—a clue—that handkerchief—

"Margaret!" Her voice sounded so odd that Maggie
dropped the pajamas and grabbed Beth's shoulders and
shook her.

"What, Elizabeth? You look like you're frozen."

"Margaret. Look at that handkerchief!"

"Well? One of Trace's old handkerchiefs he won't
let anybody else even wash or iron—not that anybody

would want to. It's not the one that was dropped under the tree, because we found that one burned."

"No, it's not that one. But look at it! The initial! I've got it! The right clue, this time."

"Tell me!"

"Margaret, I think I know now who the Goofy Ornament-Grabber is! But—it's more of a mystery than ever. I don't know why. It doesn't make any sense at all. He must be out of his mind, that's all; and if he is, Pip's in danger!"

The Mysterious SOS

"What in the world are you talking about, Elizabeth?"

"It's Trace!" Beth said. "It's got to be Trace. He's the Goofy Ornament-Grabber. It all fits, see?"

"No, I don't see," Maggie said. "How do you figure it's Trace? Why would he steal ornaments off his own tree?"

"That's what I don't know. But he had angel-hair in his pocket, didn't he? Probably came off my angel. He's as tall as Pete Abel and has light hair and an Army jacket that had the angel-hair in its pocket. I only saw the boy from the back, remember? Trace could have heard me talking about wanting my angel back, and he was the only one who could have brought it back, because Pete was watching, and nobody else came in between nine and ten o'clock. The reason Trace didn't bother to lock the door tonight when he went out is that he already knew nobody would try to get in to steal anything—he was the only one who ever had. Don't you see? That's why he was so sure Pete Abel was somewhere else, and gave him the alibi. Because Pete wasn't here when Trace was stripping the tree—so he had to be someplace else."

"Well, but at least Trace isn't all bad." Maggie spoke up for him. "He didn't want to let Pete take the blame for something he did himself. And he brought back your angel when he found out how much it meant to you. He probably wouldn't have taken it if he'd known. But why on earth would he—"

"He's got to have flipped," Beth said positively. "Nobody in his right mind would have done it."

"What about the handkerchief clue?"

"That's what gave me the answer, except of course I don't know why yet. We'll have to find out why, because I can't just say it was Trace instead of Pete. Mama will say I'm jumping to conclusions again, and Champ might think it's just because I didn't like Trace much for a stepbrother when he came here—and because I wanted so much to clear Pete."

"How did the handkerchief clue give you the answer? We found the handkerchief burned. And Trace's name doesn't begin with a *Z*."

"Trace could have got it out of my drawer easily and burned it right there. And his name doesn't begin with a *Q*, either," Beth said triumphantly. "That was how I finally guessed the answer. See this?" Out of the pile of laundry she picked the handkerchief she had spotted, and held it out for Maggie to see. In the corner was an embroidered *Q*. "It kept bothering me, until I connected it with something else in my mind. Hardly anybody has a name beginning with *Q* or *Z*, right? So probably at sales, stores have—cheap—lots of nice new linen handkerchiefs that nobody buys because of the odd initials. Trace's mother liked to buy bargains, and she would have figured that it didn't matter what initials they had; he could blow his nose on them just as well. So she bought him some bargain handkerchiefs. Get it?"

"I get it!" Maggie said excitedly. "But now we've got to find him and ask him why he took the stuff. And see if Pip's with him—or if she really was kidnapped."

"Maybe he'll take care of her, even if he is out of his mind," Beth hoped. "He's always seemed to love Pip; that's one good thing about him."

"Come on, Little Dog, smell these pajamas and find him!" Maggie gave Little Dog a good smell of them and then ran down the stairs. Both girls put on coats and mittens and wrapped wool scarves about their ears. The snow was coming down faster now, and sticking, but they didn't have time to stop and admire it.

Maggie's hand in her coat pocket encountered Useless' collar that Little Dog had found. "I've got an idea," she told Beth. "Why don't we start looking down in the field where Useless' collar was? That cat probably went down there after Pip; he always followed her wherever she went."

"Good idea." Beth praised her. "Maybe we ought to change his name to Useful, instead, if that helps find her. We don't know where else to start hunting them, so we might as well start there."

The snow was dotting the air with white now, clinging to leaves and settling softly in the bare black forks of trees, as they ran down the street toward the big open field between Ginny's grandmother's house and the railroad depot, closed now that the last train had gone by. Little Dog risked his feet doubtfully on the unfamiliar cold white covering that cushioned the sidewalk. That slowed him up. The whole world seemed more silent because of the snow. Silent Night. Then in the distance the church bells began to chime out Christmas carols. "O little town of Bethlehem," they rang. "How still we see thee lie."

"It's like Pleasant Grove was Bethlehem," Maggie said, panting. "It's all so quiet. I wonder if anybody's baby will be born tonight?"

Little Dog got used to the snow and caught up with them before they had gone the three blocks to the big field. He ran ahead and began to bark, destroying the whispery stillness that enveloped the silvery chimes.

"What's he barking at?" Beth wondered.

"Why, look, Beth! It's Useless. There in the field—"

"Maybe he followed Pip. Maybe Pip's there asleep under the snow like those kids we read about in that old story."

They rushed to where Useless was sitting on his haunches in the snow, his tail curled around his feet, his green eyes mysterious—not communicating anything at all except that maybe he had followed Pip.

"She's not here."

"You didn't really think—"

"No, I never did believe that about kids sleeping under the snow like a blanket anyhow. Most kids would have had better sense than that. Even if snow does make a good blanket for daffodil bulbs, like Mama said. It sure wouldn't feel like any blanket I ever felt."

"Maybe we ought to go ask at Ginny's grandma's if they saw Pip and Trace anywhere."

"There's a light in their house now. Don't their wreaths look pretty?"

As they started toward the house, however, they heard something that stopped them.

"Listen!" Beth stood still and fumbled at her scarf with her mittened hands, to uncover her ears. "I thought I heard something."

Maggie uncovered her ears too. "It sounds like—the bells almost drown it out but—"

"It sounds like Trace's Boy Scout whistle!"

Over in the field near the railroad the old tower stood dark and lonely. But from somewhere came very faintly, almost drowned by the wind and the chimes, the sound of a shrill whistle blowing and stopping and blowing again.

"It's—I think it's making those dot-and-dash signals!" Beth said. "It's blowing long whistles and short
ones. He's got to be somewhere—and it might be the lab
after all. It looks so dark and deserted, though—
doesn't look like anybody could be there. But he's
somewhere around here, and that whistle is trying to
tell somebody something. Maybe he's trying to tell

where they are. Maybe the kidnappers have locked them up somewhere and that's the only way Trace can call for help. Margaret, run to Mr. Marvell's house and get him to come tell us what message Trace is sending. And get Chief Steadman, if you can find him, and anybody else who can help, while I keep looking around here for Pip and Trace. We might need to hurry, before the kidnappers get back or something. Take Little Dog to protect you, in case they're on the way back and you might meet them!"

"I thought I heard something over there in the bushes!" Maggie said fearfully. "You oughtn't to stay here by yourself, Elizabeth. Come with me. We haven't seen anybody outdoors around here at all that you could call if—"

"Are you chicken? Scared to go by yourself?"

"No-o-o-o—"

"I'm the oldest and you have to do what I say. So go!"

"I'll go. But you be careful," Maggie said, starting to run, calling Little Dog, who followed, scattering snow.

"Hurry!" Beth called after her. "If you can't find Mr. Marvell and Chief Steadman, bring somebody!"

She really was sort of afraid to stay there by herself, because it was a lonely spot after the ticket office closed, and Ginny's grandmother's house was quite a long way from the railroad station; and that field looked enormous right now. But she dimly remembered something about the dots and dashes the whistle was making—they were three shorts, three longs, and three shorts. Beth was pretty sure they meant SOS. Help!

Pip and Trace must be in danger! They might need help before Maggie could get back with anybody. Beth thought of running for help herself, but before she could carry out this idea she glanced up again at the windows of Trace's lab at the top of the dark tower. And now that she was looking more closely, she thought she could see a thin line of light, as though the windows were covered with something that left only a bit of the light showing at the edges.

Yes; now she was positive. There was somebody up there in the lab, and it might be Pip and Trace. And the whistle kept on sounding—urgently, she thought now. Desperately. She couldn't imagine how Trace could be free to blow a whistle and yet not be free to come down, but clearly he needed help. For Pip. Something might be happening to Pip this very minute. Beth couldn't wait for somebody else to do it. She had to go and help them herself.

Wrapping her scarf more tightly about her head, she started toward the tower. Snow was swirling around it now. Panic caught her; she felt more like running in the other direction. She was shaking all over, and not just from cold. Her heart was pounding hard. Her feet and hands were icy. When she reached the tower, she could hardly grasp the railing.

But she put her foot on the first rickety wooden step, slippery with snow, and started to climb.

Danger
in the
Old Tower

The narrow steps zigzagged up one side of the tower, and now, standing on them, Beth couldn't even see the windows of the hut. When she looked up, she saw only the smooth shaft of the round tower rising high above her, with the next zigzag of the steps over her head, and high above that, the platform's bottom. As she climbed higher, she didn't dare look down.

The wind whipped the snow about her, and pushed her against the cold cement. She tried to steady herself against that frigid surface with her left hand while she held onto the railing of the steps with the other. But the steps were rather far apart, with no solid risers—just vacant spaces through which a foot might go if the climber slipped—and she didn't feel very sure-footed.

Beth and the steps both shivered in the wind. Her nose ached with cold. She found she could hardly grasp the railing at all with her mittens on; so she took off the one on her right hand. Her fingers soon got stiff and numb, but she could hold on a little better without the mitten, while she moved carefully up the steps.

The sound of the whistle was closer now. She was practically certain it was the SOS call. And also the groups of three shrill sounds seemed to be saying, "Hurry up! Hurry up! Hurry up!"

Now she was about halfway to the top, clinging to the rail with one hand and pressing the other against the icy cement of the tower. She was on the side of the tower toward Ginny's grandmother's house. Her eye caught the friendly light now showing in their kitchen window, and fleetingly she wished Ginny or her brothers—she knew they were at their grandmother's for Christmas—might look out and notice that there was a kid hanging onto the tower steps. But the night was so dark now that they surely couldn't even see the tower. They were probably busy cooking supper and not even looking out to see the drifting snow. Any other time Ginny's kid brothers would have been out playing in the snow, but now, when she needed them there, they weren't. She remembered hearing that little Jack had a cold, so more than likely their grandma wouldn't let him and George out to play in the snow at all. Funny what silly, unimportant thoughts you could have when you were in a terrible spot like this. She knew she ought to be thinking about Pip, instead of about Jack's bad cold. But you couldn't help what came into your mind.

What was that? She thought she heard a sound below her on the steps. As though a foot scraped and a wooden step creaked. She hadn't looked down before,

because it would make her dizzy. Now she had to risk
a look.

She turned, and the wind nearly swept her off her
feet. Swirling snow beat her with soft whips. It was
dark down below her.

But there was somebody else on the ladder-like
steps.

She could see a tall dark shadowy someone hanging onto the railing, climbing up behind her faster than she was climbing. She screamed, but the wind carried the scream high and away. The threatening form below yelled something back at her too, but she couldn't hear anything but the sound, not words. Whoever it was, was gaining on her. Panicky, she tried to climb faster.

Her foot slipped. She was down on her side on the narrow rung, perilously hanging onto it, trying frenziedly to scramble back up. But her chilled hand could hardly grasp the railing. She screamed again, but she knew no one could hear her. There hadn't been time for Maggie to get anyone yet.

The dark shape below was almost up with her now. Beth shut her eyes and mentally begged for help. In her panic she couldn't even remember any prayers. All she could think of was "Little Lord Jesus asleep in the hay." That wasn't exactly a prayer. But she said it silently. It might work like a magic spell to keep away harm.

Then she felt a strong, rough hand catch her and pull her onto her feet again, and an arm around her back, steadying her. And a rude voice said, "What do you think you're trying to do, anyhow? I thought even girls had more sense! Trying to climb a thing like this on a night like this—"

She turned her head, and in the dimness she saw that it was Pete Abel behind her. Goldie had said he sometimes followed her and Maggie, she remembered. He must have made the noise that Maggie had heard in the bushes. He must have been there under Ginny's grandmother's magnolia trees when Beth started to climb.

Well, she wasn't afraid of Pete Abel, now that she knew it was Pete. He surely didn't have it in for her enough to push her off the tower.

"I've got as much right to be here as you have," she retorted.

"Don't be a dope," Pete said. "I'm freezing. Come on down. I'll help you get down without falling. I'd help even a cat if it got stuck in a tree and couldn't get down."

"I'm not stuck. I could get down all right," Beth said scornfully, feeling braver now that she wasn't by herself. "I was trying to get up there, not down."

Hanging on to the railing in the cold, her teeth chattering against each other, Beth tried to think things through. She had to make a quick decision whether to trust Pete or not. He couldn't be here for any reason

but to try to help her down. Even though Beth was
the one who had got him in trouble. So he wasn't—at
least right now he wasn't—trying to hurt her. She decided to trust him. She had to. Because Pip and Trace
needed help, and maybe Pete would help if she begged
him.

"Pete," she appealed, "please, will you help me get
to that platform up there so we can see what's happening and try to keep it from happening if it's something
bad? You see, Pip might have been kidnapped, and I
think Trace is with her and that they're up there.
There's a dim light behind that dark thing that's over
the window. Can't you hear the whistle whenever the
wind lets up for a minute? That's Trace making dot-
and-dash signals with his whistle. I don't know how
he's doing it, but Trace is a genius. I think it means
SOS—and that means 'Help!' I haven't got time to tell
you everything now, but I think we've got you cleared
on the Christmas tree thing—Maggie and I. But we
don't know the whole explanation yet. Anyhow, we've
got to help Trace and Pip. I sent Maggie for help, but
they might be in danger—in some real bad spot. I
can't wait till she gets back. So, will you help me?"

Pete hesitated only a minute; then he said, "O.K., go
ahead. I'm right behind you. I'll catch you if you
should slip. Go on up as fast as you can!"

Beth breathed, "Oh, thank you, Pete—" and started
to climb confidently, now that he was behind her.

They reached the shaky planks that made the platform for the shack that was Trace's lab. "Let's sneak around to the window," Beth whispered to Pete, who seemed an ally now instead of somebody who hated her, "and look under that black thing over the glass and see if we can find out what's going on in there."

"O.K.," Pete said. "Hang on. It's a long way down if we fall."

They inched their hazardous way around to the first window. It was about as high as Beth's shoulders. As she had hoped, the edge of the glass was not quite covered, and she could see into the small, dim room. Pete put his eye to the other side.

The first thing Beth saw in the flickering light was a Christmas tree. A little one, a short-leafed pine. The one—she was suddenly sure—that had been cut in the lot behind their house. There was no electric light in the room, but she could make out the ornaments on the tree—the ones that had earlier been on the tree at home. The German bird in the nest, and the silver pine cones, and the others— She could see them because there were candles on the tree, and they were lighted—and they were so beautiful! Just like that old-fashioned Christmas card.

And there were toys under the tree—a medium-sized doll, a doll's cradle, a xylophone, a paper-doll book, and a stuffed cat.

Then she saw Trace. He wasn't blowing the whistle,

and yet it was still sounding. She wondered how he had managed to make it do that. But he was awfully smart, Mr. Marvell always said, about fixing up such tricky things electrically. That old vacuum cleaner of Mama's could blow instead of suck if you reversed it, she remembered. Probably he had the whistle hanging outside, attached to an electric battery inside, set some way so that the vacuum cleaner would blow the SOS call at intervals.

Anyway, Trace wasn't blowing the whistle, but what he was doing was so amazing that Beth caught her breath. She felt tears coming, and she knew they'd freeze on her cheeks if she cried.

Trace was sitting on an upturned box. He had Pip between his knees, and he was trying to fix her blond hair in a ponytail the way she wore it. He wasn't making a very good ponytail; it was all crooked and clumsy. But he wasn't jerking her or being impatient with her. He seemed to be talking softly to her, being very gentle with her—and Beth had never seen this side of Trace before. He didn't act like that at home, ever—not even with Pip. I guess, Beth thought, it's because Mama takes care of Pip and he doesn't have a chance.

Then Beth twisted her head around with her cheek almost flat against the glass so she could get a glimpse of the other side of the room beyond the Christmas tree —the side with the door that was the only way to get in or out of the lab. She caught her breath again, from astonishment. She heard Pete say, "This is the craziest—"

It really was. Right across the door was Trace's cot that Mr. Marvell had lent him for his lab; and on it lay a woman Beth had never seen before. She wasn't asleep; Beth could see her eyes glitter in the candlelight. She seemed to be watching Trace. She looked sort of—wild. Now Beth realized that the woman was blocking the way out, that she wouldn't let Trace and Pip go. Was she the kidnapper? How did she keep them there if they wanted to get out? And why? Trace was surely stronger than the woman; she looked thin and sort of frail.

Then the answer—or part of it, anyway—nagged at her understanding. The woman had blond hair, like Trace's hair and Pip's. Hers was straggly and not combed, but it was blond. Did she look like Pip? Did Trace have a nose like hers? Was she Phyllis? Their mother? Then what was the matter with her? She didn't look like anybody's mother Beth had ever seen. She looked awful.

Now Trace tied a blue ribbon awkwardly on Pip's crooked ponytail, and gave her the doll from under the tree to play with. She sat on the box and cuddled it, but she watched Trace as he went over to the cot and began talking with the woman. Beth couldn't hear what they said, but it was clearly an argument.

But why had he got himself in a spot like this any-how? And Pip too? Beth tried to reason it out, fast. Well, if the woman was his mother—he had been so crazy about her that he must not have known she was like this. She probably wasn't when she lived with them; or perhaps Champ had somehow managed not to let the children or anybody know about it.

Maybe she had kept in touch with Trace all this time, and maybe she had told him she couldn't stand the thought of Christmas without her children. Maybe Trace had thought he could keep her hidden in the tower—that would explain the food missing from home —and fix up the Christmas tree so she could have Christmas the way she used to, with him and Pip. Maybe she had promised to go away and not let any-body know, if he would let her see Pip.

But there was that odd phone call the night Trace had slipped out of the house; she must have started to get in touch with Champ. Trace must have been trying to get her back up in the tower before anybody in town saw her. She'd have had to be using a pay telephone. And when he took her back to the tower that night, that must have been when he got the angel from the little tree, and returned it to the tree at home.

Beth could understand now why Trace might think he had to take the ornaments. Maybe he had spent all his Christmas money for the toys to go under the tree for Pip, and maybe even for a present for his mother, and for the candles (wonder where he found candle-holders? Maybe his mother brought them and some other stuff they used to have a long time ago?) Probably he didn't have any money left when he thought about needing ornaments to go on the tree. And of course he'd want to use the old ones they had always had, like the German bird.

But why wasn't his plan working out? Why couldn't they have had the Christmas tree and the presents, and then why couldn't his mother have caught the bus and gone back to Oklahoma to where her sister, Trace's Aunt Jo, would take care of her, and have left the kids to have their regular Christmas at home with Champ and the family? Now she wouldn't let Trace and Pip get away from her in the tower. What was the matter with her anyhow? Why didn't he just push her aside and go?

As if he were reading her mind, Pete answered her question. "She looks like she's on bennies, to me," he muttered.

"Bennies?"

"Pep pills. You've heard about drug addicts, haven't you? She's been taking something—look at her eyes. And if you take a drink or two or three on top of them—well, you're way out. Off your rocker. Pa used to drive a truck, and a good many truck drivers take bennies to help them stay awake on the road. But too many of those things—and a few drinks—and you've had it. You need a strait jacket. You could die, or kill somebody, and not even know what you were doing."

"Like marijuana or LSD." Beth understood now. "So that's why Trace is sounding the SOS. He must realize she could do something dangerous to Pip. Maybe she threatened to, if he tried to take Pip away from her."

"Who is she anyhow? You think she kidnapped the kid?"

"Well, she could have. But what I think is, she's their mother—the one who got divorced—and you can see why the court gave them to Champ. Anyhow, if she's dangerous, I think we ought to try to help them get out. It might be too late when Maggie brings help. I'll explain it all to you later, Pete. But let's try to get in there now. I'll bet you and I and Trace together could make her let them go."

But before they could move away from the window, Trace suddenly dragged the cot from across the door, and the woman rushed to Pip and grabbed the child up in her arms. Trace tried to take Pip from her, but she held on, struggling to reach the door. Horrified, Beth gasped, "She's—you know what she's doing? She's threatening to jump off the tower with Pip in her arms! If she can't have Pip, she's telling him nobody can have her!"

"How do you know?"

"I just know. I could almost hear her scream it.

Maybe I can read lips and don't know it. But anyhow, that's got to be what she's told him she'll do. That's the danger."

"I guess it is," Pete conceded. "People crazy with stuff like that don't know what they're doing."

"Let's work our way around the tower to the door. Maggie ought to be here soon with some help."

"But even if the whole town's here—down below— that won't keep her from jumping if she wants to kill herself and the kid."

"So let's go in there and at least get Pip away from her!"

Beth was nearest the door. She inched her way around the rickety platform, Pete behind her. Now she was at the door. Was it locked? She pushed against it and it opened, just as the worst happened.

In trying to keep Trace from taking Pip out of her arms—and Trace was fighting her desperately for the child—the woman brushed against the tree and tilted it. Beth saw the scene as if she were in a nightmare in which she couldn't move a muscle. She saw the lighted candles fall sideways, and the flames lick like red-and-orange-colored tongues at the pine needles.

The paper chains Maggie had made caught fire and gave a vivid light. One of the glass ornaments popped with a sound like a firecracker.

Then suddenly the whole corner of the room was in flames.

The Rescue

Beth felt herself trying to go through the door into the blazing room and not being able to. She heard herself screaming. Now she was hot instead of cold—the heat was scorching her eyes.

"Get out of the way!" Pete's voice was rough in her ear. "Let me get in there—"

He pushed her back and plunged past her. She saw him reach for Pip, while Trace was struggling with the woman. Trace pinned one of her arms back and Pete snatched Pip and tore her loose from the enclosing arm. Pip was sobbing, terrified. In that curious clarity of vision that comes with crisis, Beth noticed that Pip still clung to her doll. And that the woman was crying, pitifully, heartbrokenly, her face crumpled up the way Maggie's was when she cried.

"Bring her out!" Pete hollered to Trace. "I'll take the kid down. Hurry. This old wooden shack is the kind that burns fast. The steps might catch on fire too."

"She's going to jump off!" Trace cried out in an-

guish. "She said she'd jump if anybody took Pip away
from her! She's—she's my mother! And she might
jump and be killed—"

Pete was already out the door and starting around the
platform to the steps, with Pip screaming and struggling in his arms. Beth shouted to Trace, "Try! Try!
Maybe she'll come. Maybe she won't jump. You've got
to take the chance. Try! You've got to get out of there.
You'll burn up, Trace! The platform will catch fire in
a minute—and then the steps will go—"

He struggled with his mother, trying to drag her out,
while the flames singed the woman's wild hair and
nipped at Trace's shoes. The floor was on fire.

Beth heard, without being really conscious of hearing it, the sound of the siren that called out the Volunteer Fire Department. She wanted to run somewhere,
to leave the dreadful scene, to save herself no matter
what happened to Trace and his mother. But she
couldn't. She was rooted there, still in her nightmare,
and dimly aware that she couldn't abandon Trace
when he was in such a spot. But all three of them were
going to be burned to death if they didn't get out.

Then she remembered something from last summer,
from the lifesaving class at the swimming pool.
"Trace!" she screamed shrilly above the roar of the
burning board walls. "Hit her! Hard! Knock her out!
You've got to. It's the only way to save her, don't you
see? Hit her on the chin! Do it! You've got to!"

Trace heard her. Beth saw him draw back and then lunge toward his mother, striking a hard blow to her face. She crumpled, and he caught her up over his shoulder and staggered out the door, hurrying to the steps. "Come on!" he ordered Beth.

She followed. Trace's mother was so skinny, she noticed, that he could carry her easier than Pete was carrying Pip. Where were Pete and Pip now? She looked down.

There was a crowd of people down there. She wondered if Maggie had brought them, or if they'd seen the fire. They must have seen it, because the Volunteer Fire Department was there, with the fire engine and all. They were spreading nets on both sides of the tower. That's in case one of us falls, she thought dully, or the steps catch on fire and break before we can get down.

Trace was feeling his way down the steps, his mother's head hanging limp over his shoulder. Beth was close behind him. Further down the steps Pete was trying to manage Pip, who was fighting him so he could hardly hold her.

Suddenly, there was a crash above, and Beth felt hot bits of wood or ashes or something falling around her, touching her bare hand with points of fire at the same time snow was touching it with bits of wet.

Trace hesitated when the lab crashed in above, but the wooden steps didn't seem to be burning yet. Beth could hear him breathing hard and could see the fog his breath made. He went on. The Volunteer Fire Department was rushing a ladder up the side of the tower toward them, and Beth saw Mr. Jimmy, with his fireman's hat on, starting up it to help them get down.

Now Beth and Trace were more than halfway down, and when she risked another dizzying look at the ground, she picked out Maggie and Mr. Marvell and Little Dog from the crowd. And yes, there were Mama and Champ too. An overwhelming relief lifted her out of her fear when she saw them all there. Nothing bad could happen now.

After that, Beth's feet felt more secure on the steps. She hung onto the railing still, but she thought she didn't even need Mr. Jimmy's help to get onto that fire ladder. He had reached Pete and tried to take Pip from his arms, but just like any contrary three-year-old, at this point the crying Pip was hanging onto Pete as if he were her last friend. So Pete nodded to Mr. Jimmy and kept on climbing down with Pip clinging close to him.

Mr. Jimmy climbed nimbly on up the ladder to Trace, and Trace let him take the unconscious woman. Beth thought Trace looked pretty near to fainting. When Mr. Jimmy started away with his mother, he sat down suddenly on the step, and put his head on his knees. Mr. Jimmy said, "Stay right there, kids. We'll get you in a minute."

Beth leaned forward. "Are you O.K., Trace? You're not mad because we heard your SOS and came to help?"

"No, I'm not mad. Just let me sit here a minute, will you?"

"Sure. I get dizzy when I look down too. Let's wait." Trace looked so forlorn, so exhausted, that Beth moved down the other two steps and sat beside him. She couldn't wait to ask him, "Say, how did you make that whistle blow SOS?"

"The vacuum cleaner motor and the remote control out of the old TV set."

"I nearly guessed right." But she'd never know how he could do things like that, and neither would Maggie.

This was sort of like being in a Ferris wheel seat, she thought, with the people below and the cloudy sky overhead, and a few stars out. She noticed with surprise that the snow had stopped.

But overhead there was still the fire too. It lit up the sky like the carnival lights do when you are on a

real Ferris wheel. The sparks and bits of burning wood that dropped near the two of them made her nervous, but still it was probably better to wait; the ladder would be safer than the steps.

Her bare hand was cold; she wondered what had become of the mitten she had taken off. She noticed soot on Trace's hands as he held his head. She was so sorry for him that she put out her hand and touched his. And she was sort of surprised when he didn't jerk away. Maybe his hands were so cold he didn't even feel hers?

He mumbled something, and she leaned closer to hear what he said. "How am I ever going to explain it to Dad and Aunt Mary? And Mr. Marvell?"

"It'll be all right," Beth said. "They'll understand. I think I understand already, almost all, anyway. Why you did it, I mean. And you'd be surprised how much grownups can understand, if you give them a chance."

"But I was so wrong," Trace muttered. "See, I didn't understand how it was with her—my mother. Now I see why he had to— But I didn't know. She—she didn't know what she was doing. She wouldn't stop taking those pills and drinking that stuff. Most of the time she seemed all right, but then she'd get like that. She was going to jump off that tower and take Pip with her. And it would have been my fault if she had. Because I let her hide up there, and I tried to fix Christmas for her like it used to be."

"It'll be all right now," Beth repeated, trying to

sound comforting because he looked so sad and scared. "She'll be in the hospital and maybe get well for good, and then you and Pip can go and see her and your Aunt Jo sometimes. See, there's the ambulance and Dr. Barton down there now. Champ just put her in the ambulance. She'll be all right now. And Mama's holding Pip, and now Champ is coming over here and starting up the ladder to get us!"

"Aw, we can get down without all that!" Trace said. He got to his feet and brushed a hand across his eyes, and left more streaks of soot on his face. He started down the steps calling, "Never mind, Dad!"

"They've got the hose on now," Beth said. "It took a while, didn't it? Maybe the water was frozen."

He just said, "Come on!" a bit crossly.

Beth thought she could climb down the rest of the steps by herself too, but it did feel sort of good when Champ put an arm around her and said, "Hang on," and carried her the rest of the way down. When he set her on her feet beside Maggie, she tightened her arm around his neck for a minute, in a little hug.

Maggie was jumping up and down with excitement. "You've got to tell me all about it!" she said. "I got Mr. Marvell as soon as I could, but by that time everybody else was here too." Little Dog jumped up and tried to pull Beth's other mitten off. Mama hugged her as if she would never let go, and everybody else was crowding around asking what happened. Beth saw the ambulance move off, and she knew Trace's mother was taken care of—so the rest could wait. Pip was already chattering to Maggie about going home to hang up her stocking and put out cookies for Santa Claus. Little kids got over things mighty quick. Pip's mother must have seemed like a stranger to her. And that was sad.

Then she thought about Pete. "Where's Pete? I've got to tell Chief Steadman about Pete. He didn't take the ornaments. That was Trace, but it wasn't stealing because they were really Trace's—and he brought back my angel. But Pete came up those steps behind me and kept me from falling, and then he went right into that fire and rescued Pip. And everybody's got to know Pete's O.K.!"

"Everybody knows it, honey," Mama said. "We saw Pete come down out of the fire with Pip in his arms. Pete's a hero, and Champ says he's going to recommend him for some kind of a medal."

"What about Trace? He rescued somebody too."

"Well, I don't exactly think Trace is in line for any medals. Champ will probably understand and forgive him, but he's got a lot of explaining to do."

"He was just trying to give his mother one more Christmas with her kids," Beth said. "He blew it, of course, but it wasn't all his fault. He didn't know how she'd act. Maybe Champ should have explained to Trace before, about his mother taking bennies and drinking something that would hurt her?"

"Maybe so. But you know, sometimes you children aren't easy to talk to. To be convinced, you have to see for yourselves. That's the way it was with Trace. He had to find out for himself how his mother needs help. She'll get it; Champ and Trace's Aunt Jo will try again."

"Poor Trace. But I saw Champ hug him hard, so I guess maybe he won't punish him much. At least, not till after Christmas."

Mama laughed. "I'll use my influence. Maybe The Establishment will suspend sentence."

Beth hugged her again. Then she looked around. "Where's old Pete now?"

There he was, in the middle of a crowd, looking embarrassed at their questions and their praise. Champ's arm was around his shoulder and Chief Steadman was shaking his hand. Well, that was all right, then. Now Beth could enjoy Christmas.

But then she saw Trace. Everybody was gathered around, talking to Pete—and Trace was slipping off toward home by himself, with his head down and his hands in his pockets. He looked awfully lonesome. All the houses he was passing were decorated and gay, and Trace was sad.

"Come on!" she said to Maggie. They ran after Trace, and Little Dog ran too.

They fell in step beside him and didn't say a word. Beth thought that if she were Trace, she'd rather just have somebody there who wouldn't talk. Just be there. Maggie didn't understand it all yet, she knew, but Maggie had enough sense to trot along and keep quiet, like Little Dog. If they had said anything, Trace would have said, "Go away. Leave me alone."

He didn't tell them to go away. When they were nearly home, he actually spoke to them. His voice was kind of odd, as if he had just swallowed something that was hard to get down. "Aren't you kids going to be late for singing carols around at people's houses?"

"We'll hurry up and wash and maybe it won't be too late. Everybody'll know why, if we aren't exactly on time. Anyhow, they might have to go back to church and finish the cantata first."

Maggie began to sing softly, "Silent night, holy night. All is calm, all is bright—" She broke off and looked up at Trace and caught his bare hand with her mittened one. "Won't you come with us to sing the carols, Trace?" she asked. "Mr. Fred would be glad— he says we need more boys." Beth thought approvingly, That's very keen of Maggie.

But Trace said, "No."

Maggie's head drooped, and she took her hand back and put it in her pocket. He hurt her feelings, Beth thought indignantly.

She started to protest. With Christmas shining everywhere, in every house on the street, and even the stars showing now because the sky had begun to clear,

Trace shouldn't be so mean. And on Christmas Eve too. After all, they'd done everything they could to make things right for him.

But then he explained, and Beth knew she still had to work on that old fault of hers, of jumping to conclusions.

"I can't, Maggie," Trace said—still gruffly, but that didn't matter, because of what it was he was saying in that strange choked voice. "Because if Dad will just advance me my allowance and drive me over to the shopping center where the stores are still open—well, I've got a little last-minute Christmas shopping to do."

About
the author

WYLLY FOLK ST. JOHN uses Georgia as a setting for her books because she grew up loving its atmosphere of mystery and enchantment. She was born in South Carolina, spent her childhood in Savannah, and was graduated from the University of Georgia in Athens. She now lives in Social Circle, Georgia—a small town not far from Atlanta, the scene of *The Christmas Tree Mystery*. She has been a staff writer for *The Atlanta Journal and Constitution Magazine* for many years.

Mrs. St. John always writes about real children, giving them exciting fictional adventures. In *The Christmas Tree Mystery* her two grandnieces, Elizabeth and Margaret, are the children who solve the baffling mystery of who stole the ornaments off their Christmas tree, and why. As in her other books, the Georgia atmosphere is authentic and colorful.

Mrs. St. John was named Georgia Author of the Year in 1968.